# The Methuen Book of
# Contemporary Monologues for Men

**Chrys Salt** is an award-winning theatre director and writer. She is Artistic Director of 'Bare Boards . . . and a passion' Theatre Company. She now directs extensively in theatre and sound and has worked with many of the country's leading actors. She has written several books, including her popular book for actors, *Make Acting Work*, as well as theatre, radio plays, and documentaries. She is a regular tutor at the London Actors Centre.

# The Methuen Book of Contemporary Monologues for Men

Edited by
CHRYS SALT

Methuen Drama

Methuen Publishing Limited
215 Vauxhall Bridge Road
London SW1V 1EJ

10 9 8 7 6 5 4 3 2

Copyright in this selection © by Chrys Salt 2003

Methuen Publishing Ltd Reg. No. 3543167

A CIP catalogue record for this book is available from the British Library

ISBN 0 413 77292 6

Typeset by SX Composing DTP, Rayleigh, Essex
Printed and bound in Great Britain by
Cox and Wyman Ltd, Reading, Berkshire

# Contents

# Introduction

The purpose of this book is to direct you towards audition pieces that are not only right for you, but are appropriate for the audition in hand so you can bring your unique qualities as an actor to the characters you choose.

When you are called to audition, you will either be asked to read a chunk of text 'cold' for instance 'He's a Lithuanian pole vaulter with a penchant for beer . . . would you mind reading it for me?' Or you will be asked to perform something from your audition repertoire. You'll certainly need a handful of pieces under your belt whether it's the usual 'one classical and one contemporary piece' for drama school entry or something prepared for a specific audition for a theatre, a fringe company or even an agent.

In any event, it's a valuable experience to research a play and perform a speech – even if it has no immediate purpose. It keeps your mind alive and your creative juices flowing. I know one actor who learned the whole of *King Lear* – just to keep his mind active.

When you are choosing your audition pieces, think carefully about what suits you and what you are auditioning *for*. No good wheeling out your Jacobean fop for Theatre in Education (TIE) or that Berkoff monologue for an Aristophanes revival! Nor should you render your Romeo if you are fully forty-two and look like a punch-drunk refugee from *EastEnders*. Be sensible. It's horses for courses isn't it?

While I was writing my book, *Make Acting Work*, I had an interesting chat with Jude Kelly (former Artistic Director of the West Yorkshire Playhouse) about such matters. I'll quote it again because you might like to bear what she says in mind when deciding which audition piece to choose.

It's very hard to make actors understand that you are often not turning them down because they are less good than somebody else – you turn them down because they are not

. . . right in some way. Actors get very upset about this and yet if you ask them what they think of such and such a production, they often say, 'So and so was completely wrong for that part.' At the same time they will be arguing for a completely level playing field without any version of typecasting at all . . .!

Your task at audition is not only to show that you might be right for *this particular job*, but that you are an actor with talent and imagination, so even if you are not 'right' this time round you will stick in my mind when I am casting a similar role again. Remember, casting personnel probably don't have a file for 'good actor'. How could they keep track? But they might have one for 'tough cop', 'northern lad' or 'city trader'. And they'll want to keep you on file if your work has impressed.

Some parts fit like a good pair of jeans. They are comfortable. They belong to you. Something inside you keys into the character's soul. The feelings he expresses, the language he uses. His class. His agenda. It just feels 'right'. The text comes 'trippingly off the tongue'. You have the right physical equipment. These are the pieces to go for. You may be wearing them for some time. Make sure they fit.

An audition piece should be a little artefact in its own right. Sometimes (heresy oh heresy) you won't need to read the play. Taken out of context you can make it your own. I recently snaffled a piece from an old Emlyn Williams play *The Corn is Green* (set in a Welsh mining community). Out of context, with a bit of tinkering and an alternative 'back story', it worked well for an Irish actor with a line in IRA terrorists.

On most occasions, however, it's *vital* to read the play. And don't read it once, read it several times. There's an apocryphal story about the actor who goes into the radio studio to read *A Book at Bedtime*. He hasn't read the book and thinks he can wing it. It is only when he gets deep into Chapter 1 that he reads 'said Stephen with his customary lisp . . .'. He hadn't done his homework; do yours.

A couple of minutes is a short space of time for you to 'strut your stuff' so here are a few tips I hope you will find helpful. Bear them in mind in conjunction with the commentaries I have written when you are doing your study.

- Find out every last thing you can about your character and his journey. Look at the writer's stage directions. They will give you valuable clues. What do other people have to say about him? What has happened to him? What drives him? What does he want? Where has he come from? Where is he now? Church? Park? Office? Prison cell? Who is he talking to? What's their relationship? Why is he saying this now? What is the style? What's the period? What does he do for a living? What's he wearing? Suit? Doublet and hose? Trainers? Everything makes a difference. Rigour is the name of the game. Play the situation. Play the intention. The text is just the icing on the cake. If I say 'You have lovely brown eyes' am I making an observation, admiring your physical attributes or telling you I love you? How many other things could it mean? Try it using a different subtext each time. You'll see what I mean.
- Never watch yourself in the mirror or listen to yourself on tape. You'll end up trying to reproduce that magic gesture, that meaningful inflection. Unless you engage with the character afresh each time, your audition piece will become a stilted, stale affair – all form and no content.
- Practise your pieces regularly so you are not caught on the hop when the phone rings.
- Don't let nerves carry you off. Fear is the enemy and will spoil all that beautiful work you did in the bedroom. If you don't get this job, you won't lose a leg. Get your audition in perspective. Remember, if I've asked to see you, I *want* you to be good. It would be such a relief to cast this part, fill this course or take you on as a client. Do me a favour and give yourself a chance. Take some time before you begin. Close your eyes for a few moments. I'm happy to wait for your good work. Breathe deeply. Engage with your character. Exclude the paraphernalia of the audition situation from your thinking. You are no longer in a cluttered

office at Television Centre or facing a battalion of watchful faces. You are on the battlefield at Agincourt. Or facing the son you abandoned twenty years ago. You are not here to show how clever you are. You are not *showing*, you are *being*. You are here to bring two minutes of your character's breathing life into my room. The ground under your feet is the ground he walks on. You have slipped into his skin. You wear his life. Your have transformed.

- Wear something you feel comfortable in. Those biting new shoes will distract you from the job in hand. Dress appropriately. Foolish to wear your slashed jeans for that solicitor, or those leathers for a poetic hero.
- Make sure I see your eyes. They really are the mirrors of the soul. If you are *thinking* it right, it will *be* right. It won't matter to me how brilliantly you mime drowning in a vat of porridge, if your work doesn't have the ring of truth about it, I won't be interested.

So it's over to you. My commentaries should not be seen as 'giving direction' in anything but the loosest sense. But I have tried to give a few tips and indicators about context, interpretation and approach and point you towards a few clues buried in the language or the syntax. The pieces are arranged in an 'age ladder' – the youngsters at the beginning – so I hope that will make it easy for you to locate an appropriate piece. Sometimes, of course, a character's age is flexible and can be adapted to work for you so I have avoided being too specific. I have left in stage directions where they seem relevant. I hope you'll find this useful.

May the creative force be with you. Good luck.

This book is dedicated to all my students and friends in the profession from whom I learn so much.

Thanks are due to Elizabeth Ingrams, my editor at Methuen, for her good humour, unflappable support and insightful blue pencil and to Richard, my husband, for his TLC, cups of tea and inexhaustible supply of ink cartridges.

# Goliath *by Bryony Lavery*

**Goliath** is based on a book by Beatrix Campbell of the same name. It explores issues around community relations, the maintenance of law and order and social 'meltdown' on three rough estates. This section is called 'Law of the Jungle'. The scene is the Blackbird Leys Council Estate in Oxford, home of The Don. The Don is sixteen, or there-abouts. The writer describes him as having 'the presence of a top performance vehicle', as 'top cock of the walk, very powerful, very confident, full of energy which he contains or releases at will.' Here we find him waiting in a stolen car crowing about his philosophy of life.

The Don is leader of a disaffected lawless gang and has named himself after a Mafia chief. It's how he sees himself. He has no job yet he always manages to have money in his pocket and wears designer gear. Look how he affects a 'yardie style' Jamaican accent to make him look 'cool'. He and his 'posse' make life an absolute misery for decent people on the estate, but this doesn't figure in his thinking. He is 'a hard little bugger', one of the 'only mugs work' brigade – a car thief who lives the 'joy' in joyriding. The thrill of the chase and outwitting 'the babylon' (the police) is what gives him his 'buzz'. The 'rasta' rap he chants sums up his attitudes. He has no allegiances and no respect for other people or their property. His contempt for law and order is not just blatant, it's a life-style choice. 'Respeck' and power is what he craves. Two fingers are permanently raised to society. Anarchy Rules. OK? The police don't call the estate 'The Jungle' for nothing.

Being top 'bad boy' on the estate is what gives The Don status and a purpose in life.

---

**The Don**  You're afraid, fuzz.

What can you do anyway, wanker?

Upper hand, Plod.

You see a bad boy car and you say to yourself,
yeah, yeah,
I'll have some of that
I'll say to myself that if the police come
they can't catch me.
If I'm in a stolen car
the police have to be fucking good
to catch me.
The police have chased me on many occasions.

*Presses a button, rap music plays as . . .*

Ya cyan reach down pon Oxford
a driven a bran new Astra
Lef it pon de street
I man go tief it from you Rasta

A Golf GT wid a cris alloy wheel,
Bring it ere nuh man an leh we see ow it feel

De M40 is de wrong place fuh you,
Luhn a lickle respeck or me go box yah face for you

Me nuh belong to de lef
Me nuh belong to de right
Drive tru de shit in de middle of de night

*He smiles.*

chic dude
ironed tee-shirt
sharp crease in the sleeve
never a wrong wrinkle
trainers
accessories . . . scanner . . .
access to radio technology – yeah

young boy at de shop
doing a handbrake turn
pure display

de handbrake turn
but de A34 there's no handbrake turn
no spectator fe look, an no fe he learn

I'll come out when I'm ready
say eleven oclock
I can sit out there
and the babylon come out there in force
but I can sit there till two or three oclock
in the morning and then I can come out
and do what I'm gonna do . . .

at the end of the day
there is no one who goes out to display
who does not believe in themselves
that they will be getting chased
if you go out there you have to expect
to get chased
it's a educated risk

we can guarantee a police presence
we're irresistible

we just stay there till they come

the main thing is to get in there
and have one over on the babylon

lovely night

I'm the Don!
I am The Don!
I wear the trousers!
What I say GOES!

Everybody wants to be boss of something,
I want to be boss of Blackbird Leys!

# The Shadow of a Boy *by Gary Owen*

This is a lyrical play about Luke, an imaginative ten-year-old who lives with his grandmother after losing both parents in a car crash. The play addresses themes of emerging sexuality, the petty cruelties between children and a young boy's strategies for coming to terms with grief.

Comic books offer Luke an alternative world into which he can escape and dream. They contain a model of order and justice in the universe, which seems to be painfully lacking in his own life. From these he summons Shadow, a teenage emissary from outer space whose mission is to judge whether Earth is fit to join the Glactic (sic) League of Civilisation. In the comics, only one boy can see Shadow. Only one boy can show him round Earth and explain how things work. So Luke becomes that boy and Shadow a friend who says and does things that he would not dare. He embodies Luke's fears and confusions, his conscience and his emergent adolescent voice. He is a child's interpretation of a comic-book hero. He gives the lonely boy status, power and judgement.

In this speech Shadow warns Luke of impending nuclear apocalypse, articulating fears planted by feisty eleven-year-old Katie, who has told him that the siren from the local cheese factory is practice for the three minute nuclear warning. The language Shadow uses is horribly vivid, painting a gruesome picture of a nuclear attack. It gives expression to Luke's most fearful imaginings. It is the language of the playground – taunting, personal and targeted – designed to frighten and make Luke cry. Although Shadow is an imaginary hero figure he is the medium through which Luke tries to make sense of his world. He is also a character in his own right, and like Peter Pan, is spiteful, manipulative, witty and endearing, all at the same time.

Is this painful taunting the kind of treatment Luke can expect when he starts at the local comprehensive? But if the world is frizzled to a cinder, he won't have to go, will he? Shadow plays on Luke's fears . . . Nuclear holocaust or local comp? Luke can't imagine which is worse.

---

**Shadow** All right.

All right then.

It's just.

The other reason I don't think she made it up is –

(*He hesitates.* **Luke** *waits.*) – we've seen it before.

On dozens of worlds.

They can't quite make the leap to the next level – so they blow themselves to bits . . .

You wouldn't even see the explosion. There'd be a flicker of light, then the heat would burn your optic nerve away and everything would go dark.

The eighty per cent of you that is water would flash to steam. Your fat would take a fraction longer to evaporate: you might even feel it sizzle for a moment before it fell away from your skeleton.

Your muscles would char, and your bones would blacken and turn to powder, and when the blast wave hit you'd crumble and be carried up into the atmosphere, maybe right to the edge of space.

Most of the powder that was you would fall straight back to earth. If you fell on land, the land would be poisoned. If you fell on people, cancers would grow where you touched them.

But some of you would hover up in the sky for a while.

You'd go sailing round the world, till finally gravity dragged you down. The last of you would flare and burn as you fell through the atmosphere, and maybe people on the ground would see you burn, and think you were a shooting star, and make a wish on you. And if they did, they would wish . . . to be dead.

(*Beat.*) All this, from splitting proton, from neutron, from electron.

The most basic structure.

Crack it, and out comes a force.

That could consume you completely,

And leave just a shadow on the ground

To show where once a boy had been.

*He steps close to* **Luke.**

Are you . . . going to cry, Luke?

*He reaches out his hand to touch* **Luke**'s *cheek and feel for tears. Beat.*

That's a relief then. You won't have to worry about the boys at the comp teasing you for being the last one to get hairs on your willy. 'Cause everybody's hair'll just be singed off, won't it.

Only trying to look on the bright side.

# The Body *by Nick Darke*

This is a Cold War political comedy about the futility and expense of nuclear defence. A Cornish farming community lives uneasily in the shadow of an American nuclear airbase. When a local woman finds a dead body in the estuary while collecting cockles she sets off a train of rollicking, surreal and macabre events. Acts One and Two tell the same story from different perspectives.

Body was a young Marine who had been guarding the base. At the beginning of Act Two the corpse addresses the audience. It is a bright summer's day inside the perimeter fence. Body died of boredom just five minutes ago and has already come to the conclusion that dying was a mistake. He is an archetypal American soldier, tough, programmed to kill and protect the free world from the 'commies'. But after all his boot camp training he has been dispatched to defend American warheads from the sheep. There is no keen mind at work here. The ludicrous story of his enlistment is told with an absolutely straight face. Any attempt to play the comedy would ruin it. Close attention to the author's punctuation will help you find the comic rhythm of the speech and the character's lazy Southern drawl. Unhappily for Body, he finds being dead just as boring as being alive.

The speech is unrelated to the scene that follows it and stands alone very well.

──────────────

*Early morning. A bright summer's day. A dead Marine lies centre stage. Larks sing. A jet takes off and flies overhead. Larks sing. The dead Marine sits up and tells a story to the audience.*

**Body** When I was alive, towards the end of my life – by the way I'm dead right now, I died, close on five minutes ago – I had a fear of yawning. Got to figuring if I yawned too hard the skin round my lips, when they opened wide, would peel right back over my head and down my neck and turn me inside out. I started to yawn when I was sixteen, back home, when I was bored. I know that healthy guys when they hit sixteen start to do things other than yawn. But believe me, where I came from there was little hope of that. And yawning was the next best thing. One day my paw caught me yawning. He said Son join the Marines. I said Paw I'm bored. He said the Marines will sure kick the shit outa that. So. I enlisted. First thing they do is cut my hair off. Which kinda makes me uneasy cus by now I'd reached neurosis point about this skin-peeling business, and I figured the only thing which would stop the skin from shooting right back over the top of my skull when I yawned was the hair. Figured it might like hold it in check long enough for me to yank it all back into place. But on my first day . . . had my head shaved . . . believe me, I kept my mouth tight shut. But, by the end of my training at boot camp on Parris Island, I was a highly tuned killing machine, prepared to be sent to any part of the world, get shot up and die protecting the free world from the onslaught of Communism. Paw was right. Sure kicked the shit outa yawning. I was ready to kill. Go over the top. I had a weapon in my hand and my finger itched to squeeze the trigger. Got to figure if it itched much more it'd drop off. I had visions of me, under fire, storming a treeline in a fire fight and comin up face-to-face with a big Soviet stormtrooper and there I am weapon in hand ready to blast the bastard to boot hill finger on the trigger and the damn thing's itchin so much it drops off. We were issued with ointment anyhow to relieve the . . . er, but, what happens? I'm sent here. Guarding warheads. Sitting on top of that observation tower, which, thank Christ, was made unsafe by the last gale, and walking up and down the fence guarding warheads against sheep! I started yawning again. Twice, three times a day. Then it hit me. We were trained to kill, and to die. Now I dunno whether any a you good people are dead, but if you are still alive, the one thing that bothers us about dying is what happens after. I only died five minutes ago but it strikes me being dead is much the same as being alive. It's boring. I think I've bin sent to hell. Don't die. I made a mistake. I erred. It's hell all right. So. I'm dead. And in hell.

*He lies down again. Dead.*

# Ting Tang Mine *by Nick Darke*

This play is 'a parable of capitalism' set in a God-fearing Cornish tin-mining community in 1815, just after the battle of Waterloo. It is a community where fortunes are won and lost by mineral lords and speculators on the backs of hard-working miners.

Jan May is a flamboyant Cornishman in his twenties, son of a hard-pressed family who work in the mine. He is an unprincipled chancer with the gift of the gab; a master of performance. He is the kind of man who would rob his own mother, which is exactly what he tries to do when their fortunes are reversed.

When 'the prodigal' returns to the bosom of his family after nine years' absence wearing a collection of exotic ill-fitting garments and carrying a carpet bag full of cash he is greeted with suspicion. They know him of old. And it's a bit of a shock to see him. They thought he was dead.

In this speech Jan May offers his family the money, using all his powers to persuade them to take it. Look how he tantalises them with fantastical 'Boys Own' stories about his travels, castigates them for their working-class pride and religious beliefs, tempts them with all the wonders money can buy. An Eden full of apples – I'm sure the symbolism will not escape you. But his proud God-fearing family refuses to take the money, in spite of grinding poverty.

Their suspicions about Jan May are not unfounded. By the end of the play we discover his 'traveller's tales' are all fiction; that the clothes and money were found on a beach near Plymouth – after a man was murdered to get them. The lies he tells are 'fancy and fast' but like all liars he must believe them at the time of telling.

---

**Jan** *removes a selection of dry clothes from his bag. The clothes are just as gaudy as the ones he has on. He places the clothes in a pile on the bench, then tips the remaining contents of the bag out on to the ground before him. Ten thousand pounds in all denominations, notes, bonds,* *spill from the bag into a crisp gleaming pile before his family, who watch silent whilst he does this. He leaves the money for them to ponder and he changes into his dry clothes as he speaks:*

**Jan**  That's what the world had to offer me. To you, maybe, it look a fortune, but tis no more'n dust to my pocket. Cus the world's a brother to me now. I can stray out there and cross continents with ease. I've traversed whole countries without ever knowin I bin in em. I bin to places where they'd grow people to fit the mines and paint em black to save washin. I've spoke with men whose language I could never understand. Argued with princes, and popes. They tole me they was popes in a language I could never understand but who am I to question that? I debated with em and eld me ground, gambled with em and took their cash. Flirted with their mistresses! My Christ, Mother, what a vast and various herd is the human species and I tackled em all. I'm tired of adventure now. I've come ome to rest and share the fruits of my endeavour. Oh yes. Take it. Take it all. Do, take it.

*Nobody moves.*

Ten? Fifteen? Twenty thousand pounds, I haven't bothered to count it. Notes, coins, deeds, dollars, francs, pesetos, pounds. Tis all yours . . . If you're too proud to take it, Father, remember I'm your son too and I earned it just as hard as if I'd sweat down bal. Is it too much to comprehend? I can understand that. Think of it as a door, Father. A door that's opened, and you can walk through that door. And on the other side is the Garden of Eden. Full of apples. Thass all it is, Father. A door. Tidn money, tis a door! A plain old oak wood door. With perhaps a big house in the grounds of this ere Garden of Eden, Father, with exotic trees and peacocks! Or has the fear of God and the dread of Mammon bin etched too deep in ya, by the Only-the-Sobers, the Methodists, the Enthusiasts, the Thumpers, Mother, who say tis no one's right but theirs to taste the riches of this life and the poor will suffer till they die and fly to heaven? Well, I tell'e I bin all round the bastard world and there's not one dead man I've met who's happy! There's no such thing as the life hereafter, you gotta take what you can in this! I didn't cross the Gobi Desert on faith, Mother! I 'ired a camel! Thass the way the world go round!

# Eden *by Eugene O'Brien*

This is a story of a weekend in an Irish Midlands town told from the parallel perspectives of a married couple.

Billy is a 'laddish' young man, 'strapped, saddled', unhappily married to Breda, with two small girls. He is insensible to his responsibilities and can't come to terms with being wed. Billy and Breda no longer have sex. Billy seems to have a problem in that department. He spends most of his time out on the town with his mates, drinking himself stupid. It's a macho world of 'talking dirty' and fantasising about girls.

In an attempt to revive her marriage, Breda has lost a lot of weight. She's looking good. The omens are auspicious. She's got a baby-sitter. This weekend her sex life with Billy will be rekindled. But Billy has other ideas. He has his eye on the gorgeous and unattainable Imelda who reaches places Breda cannot reach. Even Tony (known as James Galway, the man with the golden flute, because of his sexual prowess) has not made it with Imelda.

At this point in Billy's story he has abandoned Breda in the pub and headed for a local party in pursuit of his quarry. He is almost too drunk to stand. Fired by desire, fuddled with drink, fantasy and reality meld as he follows Imelda to the toilet. He misreads all the signs and lunges at her. A clumsy tussle ensues culminating in Billy cracking his head open on the lavatory bowl as a crowd gathers. Breda's best friend, Eilish, who knows of Billy's sexual shortcomings, humiliates him in front of his friends by making them public. Her verbal kick is far more painful to Billy than any physical blow. It is the end of his image as 'hard man' in more senses than one.

This is a vivid narrative, evocatively told. Although a piece of story-telling, the present tense in which O'Brien chooses to tell it gives it immediacy. The actor must engage with the language and carry us step by step with Billy on his journey from sexual excitation to mortification. It is for you to decide to what extent to enact the story as Billy painfully relives it.

**Billy** So I step into her and start to chat, James Galway, and she laughs, which is great, on track, I take her arm 'cause I've so much to tell her, but she slips her arm away. 'Go into the session now, Billy.' She slips away, moves on, away from me, headin' through the kitchen, past the paintin', to the back toilet. I follow after her, the toilet door closin' as I get to it. Lean me head agin it . . . try the handle but it's locked. I so want to show her the paintin', I so want her to know about us in the paintin', so I do, I tell her about the two of us, behind the tree, me as hard as a rock, how she's kissin' me, all over me . . . how all the men in the fields workin' are lookin' over at us, because they'll all know now. That I'm havin' Imelda Egan behind the big tree and they're not. 'Do ye hear me . . . Imelda, can ye hear me,' I'm sayin' and I knock on the door, then I hear the lock. She has heard me, the lock is opening, she's invitin' me in. I push the door and there she is, laughin', sayin' that I'm stone mad. I step into her and say that I am . . . mad about her. That she's the most beautiful thing that I've ever seen and I take hold of her arm again just to try and get her into the kitchen for to show her the paintin'. I kinda pull at her, me other arm goes around her waist. The two of us agin the big tree, at last, it's how I knew it would be . . . Imelda . . . and me as hard as a rock, I must be, surely to Jeasus I must be. 'Billy,' she's sayin'. 'Billy' . . . She tries to pull away, roarin' now for me to let go of her. We stumble, we fall, in agin the jacks bowl. There's a clatter, blood comin' from me head, the singin' has stopped 'cause the men from the field come runnin' over, crowdin' into the doorway of the jacks. I look up, Eilish standin' over me, with Tony, Feggy, Brefine, the Skunk and all the others. For a second there's not a move or a word. Until some cunt lands a kick into me, Jeez Christ, Tony jumps to pull him back, Imelda frees her arm and backs off. Then I hear: 'You're a fuckin' disgrace,' Eilish standin' there, boilin'. I try to get up clingin' to the jacks bowl and Eilish is roarin' at me now, 'Big hard man, well, we all know that there's nothin' ever hard about you . . . ever.' I start laughin', at the whole thing, 'cause the boys are lookin' at me, but none of them will laugh with me, none of them will look at me except Tony who helps me up. I lash out at him. 'I'm all fuckin' right.' Eilish tellin' me to get out and go home to Breda and I stumble past her, Tony, Feggy, the Skunk, Brefine, the Cullen sisters, Imelda, the whole lotta them, past them all and out the front door, me eyes squintin' aginst the bright, me head spinnin', ribs achin' from the kick, balance goin', fightin' for to keep straight, but fall into the grate, nothin' ever hard about me. I can see them all standin' around the front door, and I'm about to roar at them that I'm all right and they can fuck off back inside, but I don't. 'Cause there's nothin' ever hard about me.

I get up slowly, concentratin' everythin' on standing, have to walk, one foot in front of the other. Faster now. Gettin' away from them now, gettin' down the town. Jack Moran is deliverin' the milk but I can't even look at him because they'll all know now, in every pub in the town, Kavanagh's, Mac's, the Corner, Bob's bar, Flanagan's, they'll all know that I'm not James Galway and that I never was.

# Roberto Zucco *by Bernard-Marie Koltès (translated by Martin Crimp)*

Koltès's young anti-hero, Roberto Zucco, is based on Italian real-life murderer, Roberto Succo, who cold-bloodedly killed his parents and a string of other people, before he was finally captured and committed suicide in prison. Koltès's inspiration was a 'Wanted' poster of the real murderer displaying photographs so different from each other that they looked like different people. Thus, Zucco is depicted 'like a flick knife – open one moment – snapped shut and pocketed the next'. Although an amoral monster, he is also resourceful, anarchic, articulate and compellingly attractive to women.

In this scene he is on a bench on a deserted metro platform in an unnamed French town. He sits next to an Old Gentleman who has missed the last train home. The station is closed and they are both locked in for the night.

The Old Gentleman is frightened by his predicament and asks Zucco to say something about himself to put him at ease.

Zucco presents himself as a 'normal sensible young man who never draws attention to himself' – a dedicated student at the Sorbonne. He postulates anonymity as the best way to live at peace with other people – to avoid recognition, become invisible. But the speech itself is a smokescreen, concealing Zucco's real nature from the Old Gentleman. The imagery of the speech, Zucco's obsession with blood, the sinister descriptions of shadowy figures in silent corridors, is fearful and disturbing. How clever he thinks he is. No one can see him, catch him or stop him. There is a terrifying inevitability about his murderous path.

Later in the play Zucco says, 'They mustn't see us – we have to be transparent. Or otherwise – if we do look into their eyes and they catch us looking, if they start to look back at us and stare, the switch in their heads will flick on and they'll kill and they'll kill . . .' Is Zucco a madman? The personification of evil? The writer makes no judgement. Koltès believes in the murderous potential in all of us.

---

**Zucco** I'm just a normal sensible young man who never draws attention to himself. Would you have even noticed me if I wasn't sitting right next to you? I've always thought that the best way to live in peace is to be as transparent as a pane of glass, like a chameleon on a stone – to walk through walls – to have no colour or smell – so people see right through you to the people on the other side, as if you just weren't there. It's no easy job to be transparent. It takes dedication. To be invisible is an old – an ancient dream. I'm not a hero. Heroes are criminals. There's not one hero whose clothes aren't steeped in blood – and blood is the one thing in the world that never goes unnoticed. The thing most visible in all the world. When the end finally comes, and the earth is smothered by the smoke of destruction, the blood-drenched rags of heroes will remain. You're talking to a student – a good one. Learn to be a good student and you never look back. I have a place at university – on the ancient benches of the Sorbonne – a seat reserved in the middle of all those other good students who don't even notice me. Because believe you me you need to be a good student – invisible and discreet – to go to the Sorbonne. It's not one of these red-brick places full of yobs and people who think they're heroes. In my university shadowy figures pace the silent corridors and their footsteps make no sound. Starting tomorrow I'm going back to my linguistics course. Tomorrow, you see, is linguistics day. And there I'll be – an invisible man among invisible men – silent and attentive behind the smokescreen of everyday life. Nothing can change the course of things, nothing. I calmly cross the prairie like a train that can never leave the tracks. I'm like a hippopotamus moving very slowly through the mud, whose chosen path and pace nothing can alter.

# Bloody Poetry *by Howard Brenton*

This is a 'phantasmagoric' drama about the relationship between the poets Byron and Shelley and their women, Mary Shelley (née Godwin) and Claire Clairmont, after the poets' first historic meeting on the banks of Lake Geneva in 1816.

Howard Brenton's character is based on the real-life Dr John William Polidori who was a brilliant, vain but highly-strung young man who graduated from Edinburgh University at the age of nineteen with a degree in medicine and speaking two foreign languages. When Byron fled to Europe following a much-publicised sexual scandal involving his half-sister, Polidori went with him as secretary and personal physician. Unknown to Byron, the unscrupulous Polidori had accepted a large sum of money from Byron's publisher to chronicle the journey. Polidori had literary pretensions but Byron and Shelley mercilessly ridiculed his efforts.

It is the night of June 18th, when Byron's reading of his ghostly poem, 'Christobel', gives Shelley a terrible seizure.

Polidori is hiding in the drawing room of the Villa Diodati and spying on the poets and their women. We eavesdrop on him as he eavesdrops on them. He is experimenting with his prose style. How will he depict this famous scene in his chronicle? He tries a hushed journalistic tone. Rejects it. Slips into more vivid imagery, then into Gothic prose before revealing himself as a miserable outsider full of sexual and literary jealousy.

The tone is voyeuristic and underpinned with resentment. He thinks he is so much better than they are. Should he portray the scene as debauchery or classical tableau? He tries on each position, each turn of phrase for size before rejecting it in favour of another. Each 'No' indicates a rapid U-turn into the next thought. He is driven first by personal angst then hijacked by his desire for posterity's kind judgement on his literary merits.

Don't worry about the other characters on stage. The speech will work perfectly well as a soliloquy.

---

**Polidori** (*aside*) I entered the drawing room of the Villa Diodati. Outside, there raged the storm. No. Outside, the storm raged. No. Outside, the storm abated. No. Outside, the storm I had just left, rolled around the gloomy house. No. No. I was wet and miserable.

*He looks around the group.* **Byron** *and* **Claire** *kiss passionately.* **Mary** *shifts towards* **Bysshe**, *turning the pages of the Wordsworth. They do not respond to* **Polidori**'s *presence.*

In a flash I saw them, a flash of lightning. The air in the room was heavy with their illicit sexuality, they had been at it, I knew it, I knew it, I knew it! They had thrown their clothes back on, the minute I came to the door! No. The two great poets, were, I observed, in contemplation, the women observing a discreet silence.

**Mary** *turns, she and* **Bysshe** *kiss passionately.* **Polidori** *flinches.*

No. The profligate would-be poets and their, their whores, lounged upon the floor, and felt disgraced at my entrance, for I brought with me the wind and the rain.

*He looks from couple to couple.*

No. I am so lonely. Why do they assume I am second-rate, when I am, not! When I am not second-rate? I mean, has Shelley ever had a good review in his life? As for my life, I have never done one thing that is not decent, to anyone; or going on middling to decent! And look at them. Byron is an overweight alcoholic, Shelley is an anorexic, neurotic mess! The planet is bestrewn with their abandoned children, lovers of both sexes and wives! Shelley has tuberculosis, Byron has syphilis, and these are the men whom the intelligent among us worship as angels of freedom. No. It was a privilege to be the friend of those two young, beautiful men, in the heyday of that summer. No. Yes. After all, I am paid five hundred pounds, by Byron's publisher, to write a diary of this summer. Dreadful time, no! Time of my life. My decent life. So!

*The couples finish their kisses.*

I entered the living room of the Villa Diodati, that stormy night.

# Shopping and Fucking *by Mark Ravenhill*

This is a blackly humorous play set in the dysfunctional world of an 'underclass' of young people whose lives revolve round drug addiction, casual sex, violence, shop-lifting, co-dependency and takeaways.

Robbie is a young gay drug addict in his twenties. The scene is Robbie's once stylish flat which has been stripped bare of anything saleable. He has just been sacked from his job in a hamburger joint after a violent incident involving a customer and a plastic fork. Where's the money going to come from now? Robbie and his flat-mate, Lulu, have got themselves in a bit of a fix. In a euphoric drug-induced state Robbie has given away three hundred Ecstasy tablets they were supposed to sell for a dealer. Now the dealer is after his money and has given the pair a week to come up with it or face the direst consequences involving a Black and Decker and their heads.

In this scene he and Lulu are selling 'telephone sex' in order to 'find' three thousand pounds in a hurry. Business is good. There is a punter on the land line and one on each of their mobiles. In this speech Robbie 'services' a religious fanatic who is into the 'forbidden fruits' of gay sex on the land line; he keeps a punter for Lulu on 'hold' on the mobile while Lulu services another client on mobile number three. There is considerable comedy to be had in the juggling of phones and the juxtaposition of Robbie's 'turn on chat' to his client (which should be a 'stimulating' piece of 'acting') and his professional 'telephone operator' tone to the client 'on hold' who finally finds the anticipation too much for him.

The actor should simply play the situation and let the verbal and visual comedy take care of itself.

---

**Robbie** *is on the phone.*

**Robbie** Come on. Take it.

This is . . . it's a golden opportunity. We could change the course of history.

*A mobile phone starts to ring.*

That's what I say. Standing in the Garden and it's: All of humanity, the course of history. Look I'm offering it to you. Because we are the first, we are the only ones. And I want you to take it.

Here in my hand. Skin. Core. Red. Red skin.

And there's juice.

And you see the juice and you want to bite.

Bite. Yes. Your tongue. The apple. Good. The forbidden fruit.

(*Answers mobile.*) Yes? For the . . .? If you can . . .? She's just. Yes. Coming. On her way. Yes.

(*To phone.*) And it's like you've never seen before, you've never looked at my body.

(*To mobile.*) If you can wait, if you can hang on. Because we're really very . . . sure, sure. A couple of minutes.

(*To phone.*) My, my cock. It's hard. And what's there between your . . . yes . . . because oh look you've got one too . . . that you've never noticed . . . yes. Your own big cock.

(*To mobile.*) Still there? Still holding? So, you're done. Another time. Of course.

(*To phone.*) And you want me and I want you and it's man on man and I'm Adam and you're Adam.

*The mobile starts to ring again.*

And you want to take it right up the . . . yes . . . oh yes . . . up against the Tree of Knowledge.

This is, I tell you, this is Paradise. This is Heaven on the Earth. And the spheres are sphering and the firm . . .

Good good.

And now we're in the . . .? Tower of . . . I see . . . the Tower of Babel. All the tongues in the world. Splashinsky. Mossambarish. Bam bam bam. Pashka pashka pashka. All right then. You're done? Good good. That's good. You take care now. Yeah.

# A Jamaican Airman Foresees His Death
## *by Fred D'Aguiar*

D'Aguiar's starting point for this play was William Butler Yeats's poem, 'An Irish Airman Foresees His Death' (which I commend to you if you don't already know it). Its style is partly inspired by this source, although the playwright uses many means to tell the story including song, soliloquy, monologue, poetry, prose and chorus.

The play is set in 1940 at the beginning of the Second World War. Alvin, a twenty-one-year-old working-class Jamaican, dreams of flying. He has been educated by his hard-working granny and has been brought up to be honest and God-fearing. When Churchill appeals to young men from the Dominions to enlist and fight Hitler it is a chance for Alvin to escape poverty, support his granny and fulfil his dream.

Alvin enlists in the Air Force and is sent to Scotland, where West Indians were sent to train as pilots during the Second World War. There he meets a white girl, Kathleen, and they fall in love. It's a relationship which endures in spite of parental prejudice.

This is Alvin's final mission, when he returns fire on a friendly plane and shoots it down. As he fires his head is full of Kathleen. Initially we are in the present. It's the heat of battle, in the moment, reactive. But this crosshatches with the past and his first sexual encounter with Kathleen, which is just as graphic. The task is to simultaneously create the drama in the air and the erotic energy of the couple's love affair on the ground. Past and present vie for precedence. Pace and tension increase on both fronts until Kathleen climaxes and Alvin discharges his gun. The plane drops from the sky as Kathleen rolls over in the bed – the 'sudden quiet' in the penultimate line referencing both events.

Observe the pause at the end when Alvin realises what he has done – his long, low drawn-out 'Nooooooo' of disbelief echoing the final throes of Kathleen's orgasm and bringing the two mirroring strands of this beautifully-structured soliloquy together.

*Rear-gunner* **Alvin Williams** *on his final mission.*

**Alvin** *They firing! They missed? Return fire! Aim! Fire! We missed them? They're still firing! Aim! Fire!* My first time I freezed up. I could only watch. She lying there, her legs spread-eagled. I wanted to touch her but couldn't. I seized up like a engine. It wasn't anything to do with her, she was lovely. It was me. We'd been kissing for ages. At the time I wanted whatever she had to offer. She tore off her clothes; I mine. We were neck and neck, matching each other garment for garment; my shirt her blouse, my vest her brassière, my trousers her skirt, my socks her stockings (I couldn't do anything in socks, I knew that much), my hat, her hairpin that let her hair fall about her shoulders with a slight shake of her head and her half-smile. We were cruising. My underpants, her panties. Us stark naked. Our shoes kicked off long ago, landing somewhere in the room with thuds. *Where did they come from! God, they missed! Fire back, Alvin! Fire back! Save yourself!* Suddenly, I freeze, like someone throw a switch in my head. All I could do was watch her, lying there, her legs spanning the bed, her hips moving from side to side, a quiet groan escaping her lips and her 'I want you'. She couldn't understand what I was waiting for. And us like two sticks rubbing together for a half-hour before, but now only she on fire, me with this thing between my legs that won't work, that could be anybody's. My first time and me only able to watch. She lying there, reaching for the four cardinal points, I mean wriggling like an eel and resembling a starfish or someone treading water all rolled into one. But I'm nailed to the spot at the end of the bed. *Aim! Fire! Bull's-eye!* So it must have clicked with her that I was good for nothing. So she just went ahead without me. I mean we had been kissing, she was all worked up. So, her hands come down her body, she getting louder and louder: 'I want you!' Her hands working faster and faster. Finally her hips rear up clear of the mattress, her heels digging for a grip like they spurring a horse, the bedclothes riding to the bottom of the bed, the bed springs crying. My hands brought to my ears, her cries still loud as ever, my eyes squeezed tight, stars swimming behind my lids till I scream stop! stop! 'No!

Not now!' she says, 'I'm nearly there!' Foolishly, I ask where. 'Everywhere!' she shouts. *I hit them! They going down! Fast!* Her knees brought up and together and she rolling on to her side. *Smoke! Fire!* Her free hand pulling the scattered bedding over her body ever so slowly, her groan low and drawn out. Me tiptoeing out, wanting to tiptoe off the world, my heart filling my head in the sudden quiet. (*Slight pause.*) No, God! Not one of ours! Nooooooo!

# A Vision of Love Revealed in Sleep
## *by Neil Bartlett*

Although attributed to Neil Bartlett, this was a company-devised piece. It was constructed around the life of Pre-Raphaelite painter, Simeon Solomon. Solomon was an ostracised homosexual – short, fat, ugly, Jewish and red-headed. Using an autobiographical style, Neil Bartlett (as both writer and performer) uses Solomon's life to recount a contemporary gay experience and access the historical reality of gay persecution. The piece borrows from primary source material around Solomon's life, Dickens, Marie Lloyd, popular song and the Bible and is underscored by music ranging from Rachmaninoff to Cole Porter. In Neil Bartlett's words 'The script . . . is an attempt to document a piece of devised gay performance, it is not a script in a conventional sense'.

Neil is a young gay man. He is naked, shaved and powdered white (none is a prerequisite for your audition). His hair is a dull red. His age is unspecified but he is representative both of Solomon himself and the imagery in his paintings.

The speech relates a gay man's journey from a club late at night and a series of painful homophobic encounters he must negotiate before reaching his flat. The stage direction is 'to talk very quietly, using a very dead quiet ordinary voice'. A good note. This is Neil's studied attempt to remain calm and stay safe. He is practising the dangerous business of getting from A to B. He doesn't stop, he doesn't look round, he keeps on walking. Look how the repetition of the phrase 'I kept on walking' and the almost unpunctuated narrative re-enforces the purposeful progress of his journey. Notice how he repeats 'I wanted to get home' like a mantra, as if by keeping his eye on this safe haven he can avoid the obstacles along his route. The almost conversational tone should indicate that such events are not unusual in Neil's life. It is the normality of his delivery and his quiet acceptance of these regular assaults that gives this piece its power to shock.

**Neil** The other night I was walking home from the club. It was one thirty in the morning; I was on my own. Where I live the buses stop at about midnight and it was Sunday night, I'd run out of money and so I couldn't afford a cab and anyway I think if you want to walk home on your own these days then you just have to practise. I was on my own there was no one with me I couldn't hear anyone else on the street and then I heard the sound of a car slowing down behind me and I thought oh no not again not tonight but I didn't stop I didn't look round because I wanted to get home and because I think if you want to walk home on your own these days then you just have to practise not being frightened so I kept on walking and eventually the car pulled up right beside me and stopped and so I thought OK let's get it over with so I stopped and turned and I looked at the woman who was driving the car and she leant across the passenger seat, she wound down the window and she said excuse me are you gay because if you are you are going to die of AIDS you wanker and so I kept on walking because it was nearly two o'clock and I wanted to get home and because I think if you practise not being frightened then it does get easier and I have often wondered what she was thinking about, I have often wondered just how she felt, I kept on walking because I wanted to get home it was one forty-five in the morning on the way to where I live there is a low wall on the left-hand side and on the wall it said GAY and I thought that's nice so I stopped to read it it said GAY, Got AIDS Yet?, and I thought that's terrible I wonder who'd want to write a thing like that I hope it's no one I know I hope it isn't my neighbours I hope it isn't the man in number forty-five and so I kept on walking because I wanted to get home on the way to where I live there's a low wall on the right-hand side and on the wall was written AIDS I thought I won't stop to read that I've read that one before it says Arse Injected Death Sentence and underneath that is written Queer Today, Gone Tomorrow and underneath that is written One Man's Meat is Another Man's Poison. I wanted to get home it was almost two o'clock I live on the fifth floor of my building as I was going up the stairs there was this man coming down it wasn't anyone I know he wasn't one of my neighbours and as I was passing he said under his breath you fucking queer, and so I got home, it was two o'clock in the morning, I got home and I shut my front door behind me. It was two o'clock in the morning, but I decided to fix myself dinner, because I think that when you live on your own, you have to take really good care of yourself.

I decided to fix myself dinner.

# Other People *by Christopher Shinn*

Stephen is a gay man in his mid-twenties. He's an aspiring actor and playwright who shares an apartment in New York City's East Village with Petra, an NYU creative writing graduate. Mark, Stephen's ex-lover and a recovering drug addict, is staying with them after a stint in 'rehab'. Stephen still loves Mark, but Mark has 'got religion' and has befriended Tan, a disaffected teenage hustler and drug dealer, a relationship Stephen finds hard to understand.

At this point in the play, the three are having one of those late night conversations friends have, each trying to outdo the other with 'horror stories' about their lives and experiences. It is almost midnight on Christmas Eve.

Stephen's story is about an audition. Notice how he recalls the detail – the glowing eyes of the blond actor (whom he obviously fancied), the cheap wood of the door, the sexual explicitness of the conversation he overhears. Look how he uses the present tense, which makes the incident feel recent although it actually took place three years ago. His feelings of inferiority and rejection are still fresh and raw. His disgust for the values of the casting personnel only thinly disguises his disgust for himself at 'playing the game': trying to be what other people want him to be – even if it means abandoning his artistic integrity in the process.

Bear in mind that the way we begin telling a story is always coloured by our knowledge of how the story ends.

———————————

**Stephen** Okay, wait, neither of you knows this one. I am at an audition for a play, this is back like three years ago, and it was a serious play, you know, really heady stuff, and I'm standing outside the room waiting, and we were to wait in this hallway while the auditions were going on, and I'm standing outside the room waiting, whatever, and I hear the actor giving his reading, of the sides. And I got a little startled and nervous because it was a very good reading, really unique and unorthodox but honest and risky, and suddenly my reading seemed so conventional. So he leaves, and he's this striking blond man, glowing eyes, very, that kind of ethereal beauty – and I say hey and he says hey and he goes down the stairs, and I'm waiting: I can hear the casting directors talking – the door to the room is made of this really cheap wood, it's like, cork or something, right? So I hear this older man's voice, middle-aged, and I hear him say, 'My God, I could fuck that boy a thousand ways to Sunday. My *God*.' You know. And this woman laughs and says, 'He is *ohhhh*,' and I hear the man say, 'And he is *stacked* beneath those clothes, I can tell.' And I hear someone else laugh. And, and then I hear footsteps, the door opens for me, and I go in, and there they are: poker-faced. And I say hi, and I meet the reader, some effeminate twenty-three-year-old, the third person I heard laughing. And I do my reading, very good, blah blah blah, good job, nice to see you, Stephen. But all I'm thinking, I'm leaving and I'm thinking, and I couldn't stay to listen to what they said obviously, there's another actor there now, but I'm walking down the stairs on to horrible West 42nd Street and it's cold and the only thought in my mind is: did he want to fuck me a thousand ways to Sunday? Nothing about my audition, my reading, my talent, my choices, no, all I could think was: did he wonder what I looked like under my clothes? And I felt soft and miserable. And went to the gym. For about a week. But. Like. I mean – it was all I cared about, would that fat fifty-year-old jerk off to my headshot that night?

# Six Degrees of Separation *by John Guare*

Paul is American, gay, black, good-looking, and resourceful with a bit of 'the wild child' about him. He is in his early twenties. He claims to have been to a Swiss boarding school and Harvard and to be the son of the actor Sidney Poitier and presents himself as being well balanced and 'sorted'. But this is far from the case. In fact he's an accomplished confidence trickster who has insinuated his way into the home of a couple of New York art dealers, Flan and Ouisa Kittredge, by claiming to know their children. Covered in blood he convinces them that his money and the only copy of his university thesis have been stolen in a Central Park mugging.

Later we discover Paul is a complete construct. A friend of the Kittredges' children has taught him how to speak and behave in society and given him detailed information about various rich people's lives – the Kittredges included. He is a fast learner and a sponge for information. But everything is fake – even the thesis that is the subject of this key speech.

The speech occurs quite early on in the play after he has cleaned himself up, cooked them a wonderful meal and helped clinch a huge art deal with their rich supper guest. Flan has asked him about the subject of the stolen thesis. There are a few clues that might have given him away. Look at the language – the slightly stilted academic phraseology, the syntax. You'd have to listen carefully to spot the flaws. But Flan and Ouisa are enchanted by his middle-class, educated veneer, intrigued by his show-biz connections, very grateful and totally convinced by his story – as we should be too.

Ironically, there is more than a slight resemblance between the character of Holden in *Catcher in the Rye* – a boy who 'wants to do so much, but can't do anything', 'hates all phoniness and only lies to others', 'wants everyone to like him', and Paul's own character. But at this point in the play, all that is to come, and the actor must not give too much away.

———————

**Paul** I borrowed a copy from a young friend of mine because I wanted to see what she had underlined and I read this book to find out why this touching, beautiful, sensitive story published in July 1951 had turned into this manifesto of hate.

I started reading. It's exactly as I remembered. Everybody's a phoney. Page two: 'My brother's in Hollywood being a prostitute.' Page three: 'What a phoney slob his father was.' Page nine: 'People never notice anything.'

Then on page twenty-two my hair stood up. Remember Holden Caulfield – the definitive sensitive youth – wearing his red hunter's cap. 'A deer-hunter hat? Like hell it is. I sort of closed one eye like I was taking aim at it. This is a people-shooting hat. I shoot people in this hat.'

Hmmm, I said. This book is preparing people for bigger moments in their lives than I ever dreamed of. Then on page eighty-nine: 'I'd rather push a guy out the window or chop his head off with an ax than sock him in the jaw. I hate fist fights . . . what scares me most is the other guy's face . . .'

I finished the book. It's a touching story, comic because the boy wants to do so much and can't do anything. Hates all phoniness and only lies to others. Wants everyone to like him, is only hateful, and is completely self-involved. In other words, a pretty accurate picture of a male adolescent.

And what alarms me about the book – not the book so much as the aura about it – is this: The book is primarily about paralysis. The boy can't function. And at the end, before he can run away and start a new life, it starts to rain and he folds.

Now there's nothing wrong in writing about emotional and intellectual paralysis. It may indeed, thanks to Chekhov and Samuel Beckett, be the great modern theme.

The extraordinary last lines of *Waiting for Godot* – 'Let's go.' 'Yes, let's go.' Stage directions: They do not move.

But the aura around this book of Salinger's – which perhaps should be read by everyone *but* young men – is this: It mirrors like a fun-house mirror and amplifies like a distorted speaker one of the great tragedies of our times – the death of the imagination.

Because what else is paralysis?

The imagination has been so debased that imagination – being imaginative – rather than being the lynchpin of our existence now stands as a synonym for something outside ourselves like science fiction or some new use for tangerine slices on raw pork chops – what an imaginative summer recipe – and *Star Wars*! So imaginative! And *Star Trek* – so imaginative! And *Lord of the Rings* – all those dwarves – so *imaginative*!

The imagination has moved out of the realm of being our link, our most personal link, with our inner lives and the world outside that world – this world we share. What is schizophrenia but a horrifying state where what's in here doesn't match up with what's out there?

Why has imagination become a synonym for style?

I believe that the imagination is the passport we create to take us into the real world.

I believe the imagination is another phrase for what is most uniquely *us*.

Jung says the greatest sin is to be unconscious.

Our boy Holden says, 'What scares me most is the other guy's face – it wouldn't be so bad if you could both be blindfolded – most of the time the faces we face are not the other guys' but our own faces. And it's the worst kind of yellowness to be so scared of yourself you put blindfolds on rather than deal with yourself . . .'

To face ourselves.

That's the hard thing.

The imagination.

That's God's gift to make the act of self-examination bearable.

# A Lie of the Mind *by Sam Shepard*

This is a haunting and unsettling drama set in Middle America.

Jake is in his thirties. He is sexist, macho, not awfully bright, unstable, given to mood swings and on a dangerously short fuse. It's a lethal cocktail that has got him into serious trouble in the past.

In this scene he has met up with his brother, Frankie, in a run-down motel. He has beaten up Beth, his bimbo actress wife and thinking he has killed her, has fled the scene in a panic. Frankie is quizzing him about what has happened.

Jake begins the speech 'slow, low and deliberate' – setting out his stall of self-justification. But the speech soon gains momentum as he starts to describe Beth's titillating clothing and the arousing smell of the oils and perfumes she applies. Everything she does is redolent with sexual promise, which he is denied. If she isn't dressing up for him, there must be someone else. Although Beth has told him that her clothes help her 'get into the part', Jake can't distinguish theatre from reality. The more he tries to exercise control and possess her, the more she seems to be laughing at him, defying him. And still the sexual provocation goes on and on. It's more than a hot-blooded male can stand.

As the speech progresses, Jake becomes more agitated until he is almost beside himself with paranoia, sexual obsession and suspicion. He distances himself from the terrible thing he has done by blaming his wife for provoking him. But however flawed his logic and irrational his responses his feelings are passionately felt and it is his inability to control them that pushes him over the edge.

(**Jake** *stays seated. Starts slow, low, deliberate.*)

**Jake** She was goin' to these goddamn rehearsals every day. Every day. Every single day. Hardly ever saw her. I saw enough though. Believe you me. Saw enough to know somethin' was goin' on. (*Builds.*) I'm no dummy. Doesn't take much to put it together. Woman starts dressin' more and more skimpy every time she goes out. Starts puttin' on more and more smells. Oils. She was always oiling herself before she went out. Every morning. Smell would wake me up. Coconut or butterscotch or some goddamn thing. Sweet stuff. Youda thought she was an ice-cream sundae. I'd watch her oiling herself while I pretended to be asleep. She was in a dream, the way she did it. Like she was imagining someone else touching her. Not me. Never me. Someone else. (*Stands, moves around space, gains momentum.*) Some guy. I don't know. Some actor-jerk. I knew she was gettin' herself ready for him. I could tell. Got worse and worse. When I finally called her on it she denied it flat. I knew she was lying too. Could tell it right away. The way she took it so light. Tried to cast it off like it was nothin'. Then she starts tellin' me it's all in *my* head. Some imaginary deal I'd cooked up in *my* head. Had nothin' to do with her, she said. Made me try to believe I was crazy. She's all innocent and I'm crazy. So I told her – I told her – I laid it on the line to her. Square business. I says – no more high heels! No more wearin' them high spiky high heels to rehearsals. No more a' that shit. And she laughs. Right to my face. She laughs. Kept puttin' 'em on. Every mornin'. Puttin' 'em back on. She says it's right for the part. Made her feel like the character she says. Then I told her she had to wear a bra and she paid no attention to that either. You could see right through her damn blouse. Right clean through it. And she never wore underpants either. That's what really got me. No underpants. You could see everything.

# Cigarettes and Chocolate
*by Anthony Minghella*

Rob is a young middle-class professional in his late twenties/early thirties. He has been in a long-term relationship with Gemma. Neither was sufficiently committed for them to live together. Much to the dismay of family and friends, Gemma has given up talking. Close friends try to make sense of her silence. In different ways and for different reasons they blame themselves.

After a week of non-communication, Rob goes round to her North London flat to confront her. He takes her silence as a personal affront – it stops him feeling special to her and relegates him to the status of everyone else. He also feels guilty because he has had a fling with one of their friends. He's not sure whether Gemma knows. Is this the reason why she will not speak?

He begins with a rather pompous rationality, which is full of studied recrimination – a thin veneer for his guilt. Then he is by turns angry, vengeful, destructive and finally full of remorse. Notice how everything Rob says is about himself and how he feels – nothing is about him trying to understand Gemma! How many times does he use the word 'I'? Although the language is 'grown-up' the sentiments are immature and selfish. The dialogue stutters out of him in stops and starts. There are unfinished sentences, repetitions and thoughts that change tack mid-sentence. He is clearly floundering and doesn't know what to think or how to respond to the situation.

The photograph he destroys at the end of the speech is of a self-immolating Buddhist monk. To Gemma it represents someone who cares enough to do something positive for change – a wordless protest about injustices in Tibet. It is precious to Gemma and Rob knows it, but doesn't understand why. It is his frustration and lack of comprehension that makes him lash out. Of course he is immediately sorry, but it is too late.

As the speech tails off into a helpless appeal we should know that Rob has destroyed much more than a photograph.

**Gemma***'s flat. Evening.*

*The* Matthew Passion.

**Rob**  I am actually very aggravated, you know. I find it very
aggravating. I find it childish, I find it shocking and aggressive, very
aggressive, actually, because you know what it says to me Gem
because by all means don't speak to the world,
go right ahead.
but with me, it says, I include you with the
others, I exclude you from anything private,
or intimate or
plus, I'm pretty certain I know what, why,
what's behind all of this, and I feel like
I'm being put in the stocks for it
so, if there is a problem, instead of talking about it
you

*The music plays.*

I don't know if you're eating, or sleeping
I don't know what you're thinking.

*The music plays.*

**Rob** *is suddenly agitated.*

what?
and please don't stare at that bloody
photograph!
because you know I have a particular
antipathy towards that picture, we've been
through this.
I don't think it's very clever, or brave, or
effective, or real, or real! to set fire to
yourself,
in fact, it's very similar,
what you're doing, what he's doing.
it's very similar,

it's like a kind of major sulk, isn't it?
in fact, I am going to burn that picture,
I should have done this the last time,

*He rips the photograph off the notice board
and holds it up threateningly –*

well talk to me then, talk to me, talk to me

*Pause.*

okay.
okay.

*He sets fire to the photograph with his lighter.*

this is just so . . .

*It burns.*

sod it
look, I'll get you another picture, I shouldn't have
done that.
I shouldn't have done that
you know, but I'm frustrated. I'll find the photograph
and get you another one.
I'm sorry, I shouldn't have done that.
Look, I'll go.

*Pause.*
*The music plays.* **Rob** *sighs.*

Gemma.

*The music plays.*

Gemma?

*The music plays.*

# Alphabetical Order *by Michael Frayn*

**Alphabetical Order** is a comedy about order and disorder and the way people get what they think they want and then discover they don't really want it. The play is set in the library of a provincial newspaper office. John is a chaotic young man of about thirty. He's Oxbridge, with accent to match, and now a leader writer on the paper. He's crumpled in appearance, rather mannered and never uses one word when seventeen will do. His connection with the world and people around him seems haphazard and intermittent.

Since Leslie, a powerhouse of efficiency and capability, arrived to take up post as assistant librarian, order has emerged from cosy chaos in the library. She has 'tidied' John into a relationship and they are contemplating buying a flat together. John is far from sure they are doing the right thing. But then John is never terribly sure about anything. Indecision is writ large as he ventures an opinion, then contradicts himself the moment it is out of his mouth, only to U-turn to his original position the minute his back is turned. Long overloaded sentences are delivered in crisp academic tones. Look how he distances himself from the argument by using the impersonal pronoun 'one'. Leslie's silences are vocal, and lacking the courage of every conviction, John reads them as dissent.

The crux of John's argument is that he doesn't want to be 'pigeon-holed' by the kind of accommodation they buy, but sadly 'pigeon-holing' is something Leslie does only too well! Does John want to be in Leslie's 'In Tray'? The truth is that John doesn't want to be defined by Leslie and he isn't sufficiently sure of his feelings to make the commitment of settling down. This manifests itself in painful indecision about the proposed flat. John would have the courage of his convictions, if only he knew what his convictions were.

John and Leslie's relationship epitomises the quest to reconcile the irreconcilable at the heart of this very funny play.

---

**John** No, I think all I'm saying is this: does one want to be quite so as it were pigeon-holed?

**Leslie** *works.*

I'm not saying one *doesn't.* Perhaps one *does.* I'm merely being a channel through which an unasked question can get itself asked.

*Silence.*

Because one would be making a fairly definite statement about oneself. Would we be as the phrase goes *happy* about saying, 'We live in a converted stable block'? Imagine what you'd think if you met someone at a party who said, 'We live in a converted stable block.' I mean, I *liked* it as a place. I liked the little cobbled yard. I liked the pots of geraniums. I didn't much like the dustbins. No, I did quite like the dustbins. In a way I liked the dustbins more than the geraniums. I thought the dustbins left more as it were scope for the imagination. But the whole place does shout as it were, 'Nice young A/B couple with intellectual tastes and as yet no children.' Doesn't it? As it were, 'He a leader-writer, she a librarian. He downwardly mobile from the upper professional classes, she upwardly mobile from the lower professional classes, both of them anxious not to define their present social location too precisely by moving into a new house in one of the carefully graduated housing estates in the suburbs.' Don't you think? Honestly?

*Silence.*

I'm not saying it *wouldn't* be right. I suppose I'm really saying that if one's going to state quite so definitely what sort of person one is, then one ought perhaps just to pause for a moment and make sure in one's own mind that one really is that sort of person.

# Closer *by Patrick Marber*

Dan is a London journalist in his mid-thirties. He's an obituarist and wannabe novelist. He meets Alice, a young stripper, on Blackfriars Bridge after a traffic accident and he is drawn to her waif-like fragility.

The play is a series of dialogues spanning the years between 1993 and 1997, which take us on a familiar journey through love, infidelity, sexual appetite and loss.

In this last scene, we learn Alice has been killed, ironically in another traffic accident, in New York. Their on/off relationship had finished some months earlier but the police had found Dan's name in her address book. Dan is on his way to identify the body and has been told she was not the person she said she was. On his way he stops to meet friends, in a memorial park. He carries a bunch of flowers.

Here, Dan comes face to face with his grief and what Alice – or Jane Jones – really meant to him. ('Who's on the slab?' in obituary parlance means 'Did anyone important die tonight?')

Notice the paragraphing. It is as if Dan's thoughts go underground then resurface in new and painful places. They come out in a non-chronological jumble – but the thoughts that link them should be as powerfully communicated as the text. Be careful not to wallow in Dan's pain. It lives in the pauses; in his efforts to contain it – in the things he doesn't say.

The symbolism of the flowers should be heartbreaking since he goes to place them at the scene of their first meeting.

---

**Dan** Jane, her name was Jane Jones. The police phoned me, they said someone I knew called Jane had died . . . they found her address book. I said there must be a mistake . . . they had to describe her . . .

There's no one else to identify the body . . .

She was knocked down by a car . . . on 43rd and Madison.

I don't know if she . . .

I went to work today . . . I wanted to pretend everything was normal. Graham said, 'Who's on the slab?' I went out by the fire exit and just cried like a baby. I covered my face . . . why do we do that?

A man from the Treasury had died. I spent all day writing his obituary.

There's no space. There's not enough space.

The phone rang. It was the police . . . they said there's no record of her parents' death . . . they said they were trying to trace them . . .

Larry was wrong . . . the scar . . . she fell off her bike.

She said she fell in love with me because I cut off my crusts . . . but it was just . . . it was only that day . . . because the bread broke in my hands . . .

*Pause.*

I bumped into Ruth last week. She's deliriously happy. Married, one kid, another on the way. She married a Spanish poet.

*He grimaces.*

She translated his work and fell in love with him. Fell in love with a collection of poems. You know what they were called, 'Solitude'.

*They laugh.* **Dan** *holds on to the flowers.*

I have to put these at Blackfriars Bridge. I have to go, I'll miss the plane.

# Humble Boy *by Charlotte Jones*

This is a compassionate comedy about Felix Humble's quest to know the unknowable and interpret his complex personal geography in terms of the laws of physics.

Felix is an 'overweight but not unattractive' man of thirty-five. He has been brought up in rural middle-class Middle England. He's an only child, prep school educated and now a Cambridge astrophysicist in search of a unified field theory. He is a brilliant intellect but finds it difficult to make connections in social and emotional situations. He has an intermittent stammer, which manifests itself mostly on the letter 'b', when he is distressed or ill at ease, which is usually when his demanding mother is around.

Felix's father, James, has been killed by an allergic reaction to his bees. When Felix returns to his parents' house for the funeral he finds family life more complicated than he can fathom.

In this scene he is in the garden talking to his mother's mousy friend, Mercy. She has asked about his studies and what he is working on.

Felix doesn't stammer now. He is on home ground and at his most confident. Physics is his passion. For Felix science is sheer beauty. He describes M-theory as if it is a finely-tuned instrument playing marvellous harmonies in his head. His enthusiasm for his subject should be infectious – his engagement, total. His quest is for what he calls that 'eureka moment' when everything becomes clear.

As Felix warms to his theme it is Jim, a gentle presence in the garden with a familiar interest in bees, to whom his words are addressed. And is it only M-theory he is talking about? By the end of the play Felix finds the connection between himself and his father and the integration with family life that had hitherto eluded him. Jim is finally able to leave the garden and be at peace.

**Felix**  At the root of everything we believe, I believe – a billionth of a billionth of a billionth of the size of an atom, so many noughts it would dazzle you – the perfect Planck length – there is a loop or a filament of energy – what we call a string – which is the fundamental building block of the universe. And these strings are stretched like the strings on a violin and they're vibrating to and fro. I know they're there – the strings, the superstrings – and that they will bring everything together into a perfect elegant super-symmetry – the jittery, frenzied world of quantum mechanics and the gentle curving geometry of gravity. You see, we know the rules for the big things like the cosmos and we know the rules for the small things like the atom, but the rules don't agree – it's the superstrings that will bring the forces together. The superstrings will give us a quantum theory of gravity – that's what I want, what we all want . . . You know, I'm so close, I can hear them! I can hear the little vibrating strings inside my head. Even though I can't prove absolutely that they're there, I can hear the patterns they're making, like they're ringing in my ears. I've just run out of the maths. The equations don't exist for what I can already sense. The excitation modes – the ringing has too many layers . . . I can't . . . hold all the notes, all the variables, all the harmonies in my head. But one day soon, I hope, I'll have it, the mother of all theories, a unified field theory. The theory of everything. And once I've done that – I'll be able to rest.

# Foley *by Michael West*

**Foley** is a one-man play about identity. George Foley, the university educated son of a gentleman farmer looks back on his life to see why it is such a disappointment. His age is unspecified but the actor needs to be able to play him up to middle age.

Foley is the last of his family, who are themselves amongst the last Protestants in the Republic of Ireland. His whole life has been a bid to escape from his family and their 'doomed and claustrophobic' world. When he finds an old pair of shoes under the bed they trigger a jumbled chronology of memories – a rural childhood, family relationships, Easters, Christmases, his father's death, a miserable marriage and conversion to Catholicism (designed to thwart his parents' expectations) and an extraordinary, life-changing encounter with a horse.

I have chosen the section where Foley and the horse first meet because it is so seminal to the play. Foley's description is reverential, you can almost hear the silence, feel the horse's soft muzzle in your hand, and smell it on the night air. This is an epiphany and all his senses are heightened.

In a moment of insight he says, 'One can appeal to the senses, the primitive triggers of smell, taste, sound . . . And if you get these right, whole worlds can open up.' Sensual experiences activate memories of events associated with them. See how the poor relationship with his wife counterpoints his perfect 'love affair' with the horse. It is the horse that will finally return Foley to his roots and his inheritance.

By the end of this moving, often funny, sometimes bitter play Foley discovers that old shoes can be better than the ones you try to replace them with.

---

**Foley** I went out for a walk. In those days the nights were dark and I walked down by the river. I walked upstream. I suppose, inland. But it felt like you were actually going downhill, the land sloping away from you, from the sea, the natural order and consequence of things. But of course you weren't.

I doubt if I can convey the thrill of those solitary walks. You were walking, you were walking quite quickly, but it felt like you weren't going anywhere, that you were treading water almost, that you were, somehow, present – that's it, that you were still, and at the centre of the world, and it was the world that was moving, almost at your behest.

Am I going too fast? Forgive me.

She always used to say I spoke too fast, by which she meant in her rather approximate style of nagging that I thought too fast, my speed of speaking being almost unimaginably constant, and in either of two modes: silence or lecturing. As she called it. Cunt.

So. Off with a spring in my step, through the streets, down some anonymous quay, fine nights, hops in the air – by which I mean the smell of hops, although I apologise, hops in the air is a rather silly phrase and somewhat beneath me. Walking for miles. Out of town. Buildings giving way to trees. Fields now behind walls rather than lots, walls turning slowly into hedges, and paths into verges, and the occasional glimpse of tractor tracks heading off to wherever their parallel business might be.

And coming one night, late, to a large rolling . . . pasture, would be the word for it. Pasture. Trees standing singly. Moonlight.

And a wooden gate in the hedgerow, the white hawthorn blossom brightening the bushes to either side.

And there in the moonlight, the smell of a horse.

The smell of horse dung actually, but it was a sweet surprise all the same. I could hear the horse breathe. That is, I could hear him before I saw him. And I could smell him before I heard him.

And there he was. He looked up and came towards me, walking full on, as if he expected me. He was grey. Dapple grey, but I couldn't see if that was because of the light, or . . . well, it's all because of the light in the end.

Do you know, when a horse is walking towards you like that, his head nodding, and his hindquarters hidden, you could almost believe in centaurs.

Although they've the wrong head . . . Scrap that.

What I recall is the sound of four hooves on turfy ground, but only seeing the front two, so the hidden back hooves hitting the sods were like grassy echoes. It was the most eloquent sight.

# The Censor *by Anthony Neilson*

The Censor is a 'suit' – middle-aged before his time, whose unenviable job it is to vet the most extreme pornographic material. He is sent a film he deems to be hard-core and 'unpassable'. Film-maker and porn actress, Shirley Fontaine, requests a meeting in his office to challenge his ruling. Her attempts to persuade him to change his mind are sexual and embarrassingly tactile. If she sees him as 'a prude, a stuffed shirt – some sort of anally retentive apparatchik' that is certainly how he appears, but there is more to him than that. He is a damaged man. His open marriage is on the rocks and his unusual, some might say deviant, fantasies have shamed him into impotency. He invites Fontaine back to his office again and again, ostensibly to give her the chance to prove her point about the artistic merit of the film. He finds her unsettling but compulsive as she moves closer and closer to his disgraceful secret. As he reveals more and more about himself he shifts from recommending a virtual ban on the film to making a viable case for its explicit sexual content.

In this speech he reads her his revised recommendations to the Board. He is pleased with himself – he is anxious to please her and prove he can see deeper than the film's superficial imagery. There is an elusive relationship perhaps between sex and love. But the academic language, the bureaucratic gobbledegook in which the speech is couched, merely serves to confirm him as a voyeur, a non-participant for whom the complex interactive quality of sex remains a mystery; something he can only envy and watch. He has censored sex out of his own life as well.

---

*The* **Censor** *is pleased with himself.*

**Censor** All right, listen to this. Are you listening?

*She nods.*

(*Reads.*) 'Miss Fontaine's intention is to depict the course of a relationship, from courtship to separation, by focusing exclusively on the couple's sexual activity.

'Thus, masturbation and oral sex denote courtship, and intercourse in the missionary position symbolises a *traditional* vow of commencement. During this stage of infatuation, with the future uncertain, the sexual activities are essentially conservative.

'But as trust deepens, and a sense of ownership develops, the activities become more various and individualised, the bodies more objectified.' – Yes?

*She remains impassive.*

All right, I don't know about this, listen to this:

'An aggressive note is introduced as the couple pass through their first *betrayal*. –

'This disillusionment opens the phase of experimentation now more animalistic, more overtly passionate and more stereotypically divided along crude gender lines.

'*But* – whilst this new element of distrust invigorates the sexuality, the spiritual basis of the relationship erodes until copulation becomes their only cement.

'As a result, we enter the realms of depersonalisation: the sexuality intensifies, becoming more abusive, more fetishistic, a rehearsal for separation. And even after this separation, they still participate in sporadic erotic encounters until new partners are found.

'*Finally*' – and this bit took me ages to get – 'we see each partner participate in solitary acts of masturbation, their memories of each other now just fuel their fantasies.' – Now *that* sounds like art, doesn't it?

*She looks unimpressed.*

So? Do I pass with honours?

*Pause.*

# Imagine Drowning *by Terry Johnson*

David is a Londoner in his early thirties. He is a journalist staying in a dreary boarding house on the barren Cumbrian coast while covering a nuclear demonstration at the Sellafield plant. He is described by the writer as 'a tall, attractive man with a dark brooding quality. He takes himself very seriously.' He has fallen out of love with his wife and somewhere along the line his head and his heart have lost their connection.

At the time the play takes place, David has been missing for a fortnight and his wife, Jane, has come looking for him. Their two stories and time-schemes interweave, as a horrific secret is exposed, and we are introduced to the disturbing residents of the boarding house. For David and Jane it is a voyage of self-discovery about the darker side of themselves and, ultimately, the workability of their marriage.

This scene is a flashback. It is the night before the demonstration. David has been to the pub with Tom, a wheelchair-bound activist. It is late at night and they are both very drunk. David pits his Thatcherite pessimism against Tom's idealistic campaigning socialism. Drink has loosened David's tongue, making him garrulous and confessional. David is a man who has lost his way. His early idealism from the days when he worked as a campaigning journalist in South Africa have come up against the cynical values of his trade. David's story says more about his disgust with himself for 'selling out' than his current political perspective.

The next stage direction gives you the clearest indication of David's angry and distressed state of mind.

———————————

*Evening.* **Tom** *and* **David** *arrive from the pub.* **David** *is drunk.*

**David** When the really bad news began . . . South Africa, 1985, I
was there. My first serious foreign assignment. If they'd known how
serious it was going to get they'd have sent someone older. Someone
like Stephenson. He was there; this Fleet Street legend, pissed old
cynic, I hated him. When the worst started there were twelve of us
in a hotel television lounge sending out the most fantastic stuff. A
dozen of us yelling down the only three phone lines. Runners
coming in with eyewitnesses. A fourteen-year-old boy dripping
blood on my word processor, I remember, wouldn't go wash up,
wanted to tell us, wanted us to tell. The din, the adrenalin. You've
never felt anything like it. Then four days later the lines were down,
metaphorically I mean. Everything was D notice. It piled up until
we stopped collecting. Material that would have made a dozen
colour supplements, let alone the actual news, and no way to pass it
out without the actual risk of actual arrest, and – we had the
evidence – of actual torture. I was desperate to get this stuff out, but
after a couple of days the hotel lounge had come to a full stop. All
these so-called foreign correspondents sitting around drinking iced
coffee. Only topic of conversation seemed to be where to get your
laundry done. Stephenson sat there. He could see I was furious.

He put down his glass, and said, 'You hear that noise?'

'What noise?'

It was silent as the grave.

I said, 'What noise?'

He looked at the dead typewriters and the comatose phones and he
said, 'The silence. Do you know what that silence is?'

I said no.

He said, 'Genocide. The silence is genocide.'

It's a very good line. Tight, perceptive, emotive. It had the desired
effect on me. I exploded. A torrent of righteous indignation. How

dare we all just fucking sit there! We are the voice of these people. It's our job to break the silence! Stephenson smiled, and passed me the phone. We had been forbidden to ask for an outside line. We both knew I might be arrested. Silenced. And I did not have the courage to pick up that phone. And I knew that my life up until that moment had been rhetoric. That whatever I believed or said or said I believed . . . it was just words. I was what mattered. The only really important thing in my life was me.

I once interviewed Enoch Powell. He was defending strong government. He said he believed that man was primarily self-centred, thus incurably greedy and inevitably violent to his fellow man. I said wasn't that a pretty pessimistic view of humanity?

He said, 'Of course. I'm a pessimist. That's why I'm a Tory.'

*A physical display of anger from* **David**. *Pent-up, inexpressible.*

# The Glee Club *by Richard Cameron*

This play is set in the sixties. Walt is a widower in his mid-thirties. He has been a miner down a South Yorkshire pit all his working life. Out of necessity his three children have been farmed out. His two daughters are with relatives and his son is in a children's home after an abusive incident involving a friend.

Walt is not well educated, but he is an honest, working-class bloke, racked by guilt at not keeping a promise to his late wife that he would keep their family together.

Walt performs with the Glee Club Singers – a group of six miners (plus a local church organist) who work down the same pit. They tour the working men's clubs with an act of comedy routines and popular songs from the forties and fifties. Not at 'the cutting edge' of music, but a 'class act' nevertheless. As well as singing, Walt plays the comedy stooge, a part well suited to his character. The bonds between the men are close.

Here, he is walking along the street at night with his Glee Club colleague, Bant. He has just received a letter from his son, which he reads out at Bant's request. The dutiful brevity, the understatement and the full signature push all Walt's buttons. He is losing his son. But what can he do? The metre of the dialogue is conversational, but look how the paragraphing indicates a painful hiatus between each thought. In spite of his bleak perspective, his loss of control after his wife died, and his self-flagellation, he is certainly not the 'cold cruel bastard' he describes. His ache for his absent kids is tearing him apart.

Walt's quest is to find a 'fairy godmother', a woman who will take him on and be a mother to his kids. He dreams of 'happy families' but it's a pipe dream that continues to elude him. And it hurts.

---

**Walt** 'Dear Dad,

Thank you for the birthday money. I think I am going to buy a fishing rod. They took us on a trip to Nostell Priory and there was a lake. I watched this man catch lots. He showed me what you do. It was great. I put a maggot on the hook.

I will save the money for when I am bigger and I leave home because I aren't allowed to be on my own by water.

Yours sincerely,

Clifford Hemmings.'

*He looks at the letter a while before putting it away.*

When Peggy died, it were just goin' to be a temporary arrangement. The girls went to my sisters, Clifford went to a friend of mine. But 'e didn't like it there. Couldn't settle. I asked him why, but 'e would never say. Frightened to. So I come to my own conclusion.

I saw this 'friend' one night, bikin' 'ome from work. I just stepped in the road and lumped him. 'E nearly finished up under a Barnsley bus. We've never spoke since.

I took Clifford away. Put 'im where 'e is.

I thought it was for the best.

You wish sometimes you could put the clock back and start again, try to be a decent human being instead of the cold cruel bastard you turn out to be. I spent my life tryin' not to be my dad and 'ere 'e is again.

Here I am makin' a bloody rabbit hutch for the widow's kids, because once in a while she asks me round for a meal and sometimes I stay when she asks me. And I'm grateful.

I've got a family. I don't want somebody else's. I want to make a rabbit hutch for my own.

The price of a bit of the other is to pretend 'er kids are mine, and while I lay in 'er bed I 'ave to pretend I 'aven't a lad of my own sleepin' in a children's 'ome dormitory twenty bloody mile away, cryin' 'iself to sleep. And the thing is, the awful thing is, Bant, I find I can do it.

# Two's Company *by Lee Hall*

**Two's Company** is a short one-man play. It is spoken directly to the audience, which always makes for an excellent audition dynamic.

Karaoke Master is a working-class bloke from Tyneside aged anything from mid-thirties to mid-forties. He is a self-confessed bigamist with two wives. Running karaoke sessions provides the perfect excuse for frequent absences from both. Here's a man who can spin two discs at once and mix some wonderful music. Or can he? There's Sheila, wife number one and her two kids in Billington and Karen, wife number two with baby Toby in Carlisle. Life is an exhausting jigsaw of gas bills, cooked dinners, kids he can never spend enough time with and long drives up the coast. But what can he do? He loves them all.

Bigamy might not be everyone's cup of tea, but as he sees it, he's not a bad man. He might be a bit 'wide' – but he wouldn't deliberately do anyone any harm. He hasn't murdered anyone has he? As long as he sticks to his rota and nobody finds out; as long as he keeps everyone happy, what harm will it do?

This section comes at the end of the play. He's telling us about spending the night with wife number two – getting up in the night to go to the toilet and seeing his baby son asleep. The sight clearly moved him. For the first time ever he felt like a dad. When Karen joins him to voice her suspicions about his double life, you can almost hear his mind going into overdrive. It's another opportunity to make a clean breast of things. But how can he come clean when the moment has passed? Denial has become a reflex. He justifies and excuses, seeking the audience's validation and approval. But whom is he trying to convince? Deep down he knows he isn't doing the right thing by either family, that by cherry picking the best bits in each relationship he's generated a lot of pain and missed out on all the things that really matter.

---

Just one little fib, that's all it takes. 'You are single, aren't you?' Thinks. Well, it's only a one-night stand. Yes. You just say yes because you don't want to hurt her feelings. You don't want to ruin the situation. Then the next time, it's worse. If you tell her now you really will ruin the day. And it goes on and on. The trouble with me is I'm too nice. The trouble with me is I just don't want to hurt anyone's feelings. And nobody's feelings are hurt. As long as I keep to me special rota. As long as I keep everything in order everybody's happy. Nobody's any the wiser.

And we went back into the bedroom. And she seemed to be happier. She was sitting on the bed smoking. And I was thinking about Tom and his flu, and Sarah and the Girl Guides. You know, seeing little Toby, in a weird way it made me feel even closer to Tommy and Sar. And then she asked me: 'You haven't got any children, you know, from a previous relationship, have you?' And I looked at her, and I couldn't think of what to say, so I said: 'No, what gave you that impression?' And she said: 'Nothing. Just something you said.' And I thought, Fuck, what the fuck have I said? So I said: 'What did I say?' 'You just once said you thought children when they were born, they were born good but the world corrupts them.' That was it?! That's what I had said. 'Is that it? What made you think that meant I've got other children?' 'The way you said it.'

A) It is unlikely that I ever said such a thing. B) It is unlikely that I said it in a way that would make somebody assume that I said it because I was already married and had two kids. So I just said: 'No, of course I haven't got kids already.'

And Karen just looked.

Was that a bad thing to have said?

# Blue/Orange *by Joe Penhall*

Robert is a senior consultant in a modern NHS psychiatric hospital in London. He is head of his department, just finishing his Ph.D. and ambitious for a professorship. Nothing must rock his boat. Christopher, a disturbed and suicidal young black man (who claims to be the son of the Ugandan dictator Idi Amin), describes him as an 'alien life form'. He is certainly alien to Christopher. Robert is intellectually arrogant, racist, jealous and self-opinionated. His understanding of Christopher's condition is purely intellectual, having spent little time observing his behaviour or discussing his problems. Anyway, it's cheaper to medicate and discharge than take up a valuable hospital bed.

Robert's agenda here is to persuade the troubled Christopher that he will be better off 'back in the community' in spite of a junior doctor's view that he is a schizophrenic suffering from paranoid delusions and needs further time in hospital. Robert's attempts to communicate with Christopher couldn't be more misguided. They reveal him as a dinosaur who has become distanced from day-to-day clinical practice by a life-style and value-system that is both alienating and inept. This is self-interest masquerading as 'patient care'. Only a recurrent speech 'tic' ('N'ha ha ha') cuts across his urbanity and suggests undercurrents of unease. Could he be frightened of Christopher? Out of his depth? Insecure about the position he is taking or simply superior? Christopher is an unbalanced, delusional black man from a sink council estate where drugs and disaffection are the norm; Robert is an establishment figure, more at home lunching at the Ivy. Does he have the slightest inkling of the gulf between their worlds?

---

*That night.* **Robert** *and* **Christopher** *sit facing each other across the table. A reading light is the only light.*

**Robert** *takes a cigarette from his pack and lights it.* **Christopher** *takes a cigarette from behind his ear and* **Robert** *lights it. They exhale.*

**Robert**  Listen listen listen listen.

*Pause.*

Listen.

*Pause.*

We all have these thoughts. It's perfectly natural. Even I have them. Yes. Me. Some days I get home from work, from a long night in the hospital, visiting, ward rounds, nothing untoward, nothing terrible, a few cross words with a colleague, some silly argument, I get home and I get in the door and I *slump*. All the life drains out of me. I think . . . Why Am I Doing This? Eh? What's in it for me? A table at the Ivy if I use the right prefix. A seminar in Norway. Some spotty young registrar takes me to the rugby and hangs on my every word. Big deal. And there are times, when I look across at this professor and that professor turning up to work in a new *Jag*, he's just come back from La Rochelle, he's off to play a round of golf at his thousand pound a year golf club, have a drink at his jolly old Mayfair club, posh dinners with drug company reps, knighthoods, appearances on Radio Four n'ha ha ha . . .

And I think . . . How do they do that?

What, are they 'experts' or something?

*I* Want To Be Professor!

What do they do that I don't?

And the answer is:

Who *Cares*? That's *their* life. Nevertheless, I feel small and I think my life adds up to nothing. And I have to keep reminding myself: Why not? Why not think these things? It's not greedy, it's not covetous.

It's *human*. It's me being a human being. And it applies to us all. And it's my right to do something about it. It's everybody's right to take steps.

But *Killing Yourself*?

Christopher?

Why?

*Silence.*

Everybody Feels Like This. At some point. In their life. Everybody feels that they've . . . lost out. It's The Human Condition. The capacity to feel *Disappointment*. It's what distinguishes us from the animals. Our *disappointment*. Mm. It's true. The capacity to grieve for lost opportunity. For the lives we *could* have led. The men or women we *may* have become. It has us in an appalling stranglehold.

And sometimes we say, Why Go On? And we want to end it all. The hell with it. Life's a sham.

*That's* human too. You don't hear doggies running about going, 'Oh that this too too solid flesh could melt.' Of course not. Why not? They're *dogs*! It would be ridiculous. Dogs have other talents. They can lick their own balls. A talent for simplicity. N'ha ha ha. Do you see? Learn to cultivate a Talent For Simplicity.

# The Lucky Ones *by Charlotte Eilenberg*

This play is about a pair of Jewish families living in Hampstead, the Blacks and the Mosenthals – refugees from Nazi Germany, and the impact their displacement has on them and the next two generations. They are 'the lucky ones' of the tile. The ones who escaped the Holocaust.

Daniel Black is in his mid-forties. He is Leo Black's son, the child of a refugee. He is dark, attractive and has had some success as an actor, although not of late. What impact might this career choice have on his bearing and mode of delivery?

Daniel and Leo have been estranged for years because of Daniel's marriage to an Arab girl half his age. Relations between them have never been good. Now Daniel has come back to make a speech at his father's funeral. He addresses the audience directly as if they are the mourners, and decades of pent-up emotion suddenly find a voice. The speech is wholly inappropriate for the occasion yet Daniel's pain seems to have a life of its own. He experienced his father as being 'angry all the time' – blaming him for everything. The child in him is still suffering the effects.

Not much in Daniel's life has gone right – his marriage, his job, his relationship with his son. The tone is edgy, full of unresolved anger, guilt and a sense of failure. The story Daniel tells about hiding in the shed where Leo kept mementos of family killed in the camps is a powerful metaphor. What would the family psychiatrist make of Daniel's desecration of this sacred place? Yet it is this 'burden of history' that extinguished Leo's ability to give his son the things he needed. In as much as Leo was a victim of Hitler, Daniel is the victim of his father's guilt at being a survivor. Are they the lucky ones?

In the introduction to her play Charlotte Eilenberg writes of 'the guilt of the (Jewish) parent desperate for their child to get it right, and the guilt of the child who can never succeed.' It is the central theme of her play and the dynamic at the heart of Daniel's fractured relationship with Leo.

**Daniel** For those of you who perhaps don't know me, I am Daniel Black. It has been suggested that I say a few words about my father Leo. (*Looking around.*) There's a lot of history here. Many of you knew Leo from the time before I was born, from the ballroom-dancing classes in Berlin. It's a measure of your – your – support for my father that so many of you – the Hampstead mafia – are here, today, for this service. I remember my late uncle, Bruno, saying at my mother's funeral a few years ago that, as you get older, there are no more parties, only funerals.

*He clears his voice, realising it's a bit close to the edge. He turns round to seek out the rabbi.*

The rabbi has spoken of Leo as a – a good man, who did his best to – to look after – people he knew. Many of us were surprised when Leo chose a Jewish service. I know that for some of you here, oldsters and youngsters alike, this will mean a lot. (*Turning again towards the rabbi.*) I think, with respect to Rabbi Cohen, my father was also a complicated man and a man of passions. You all know what he was like: everything was – life and death. (*Lifelike recreation of* Leo.) 'Who the bloody hell! You bloody clot!' If you turned the gas up a regulo beyond the one he had put it on, World War Three was round the corner. He'd disappear for a day or two and you'd think, my God he's had enough. If it wasn't perfect it was a disaster. (*Laughs.*) I'm afraid to say that for most of my life, I was that disaster.

*He laughs nervously, too loudly and too long. Pause.*

(*Deep breath. Then:*) As most of you know, we saw very little of each other in the last few years, well, ten years was the last occasion so (*clearing throat*), forgive me if I seem a little rusty . . . (*Pained.*) Now he's gone, I look at the things that kept us apart and it all does seem, well, futile, really. Becoming an actor, marrying someone he didn't – but none of that's worked out, so it makes you think, what was the point? You bloody clot!

One time he took me and Beth to the cottage that my parents jointly owned with the Mosenthals . . . in the garden, there was a shed full of his carpentry things. Children were *'streng verboten'*. I'd found out where he kept the key – I opened the door, and I hid there, in this the most sacred place in my father's world. On his work desk, I saw these faded sepia photographs of my two grandmothers, both killed in the camps, pictures I'd never seen before – there was one of my mum's mother, with grey hair, even then, she must have been in her forties, on this balcony in the 1930s. I guess my dad had made the frames . . . I heard him calling me. But I decided to stay where I was. I even – I was only nine or ten – I don't know why, it's embarrassing to say it – but I peed in the corner. Dr Feinstein over there will no doubt give his analysis later on, but I've often wondered if part of me was hoping that this time it would be different, he wouldn't be angry, that he'd show me how to make a box, or a piggy bank or something. It was terrible. By the time he'd thought of looking in the shed the police were there and everything. (*Increasingly pained.*) He flung open the door, his hand raised like this . . . Somehow we'd both failed. And we both knew we'd both failed. This was a failure we were locked into all our lives . . . Although I know, like so many of you present, Leo carried the burden of history on his shoulders – so did we – in a way.

*Pause as he recovers composure.*

Anyhow, Rabbi Cohen, Dr Feinstein, everyone, that's how I'll remember my father. Full of those intense, complicated passions that always drove him.

Tante Anna has always been very close to our family. Beth and I grew up together. Ideas, life, people, these things happened at the Mosenthals. Just as they will this afternoon: we hope that you can join us there – and have some snacks and drinks – after the service is over.

Thank you.

*Blackout.*

# Overboard *by Michel Vinaver*

This 'corporate comedy' was written at a time when the author was working as managing director of Gillette and attempting to rationalise the life of 'Vinaver the industrialist' with 'Vinaver the writer'. It stages the world of big business in the sixties at a time when big fish multinationals were swallowing industrial minnows. The seven-hour text borrows its six-movement structure from Greek Comedy, but owes as much to painting, poetry and musical composition as it does to dramatic construction, using dance, jazz and a multiplicity of cultural reference points to punctuate and amplify.

Benoît Dehaze is the business manager of Ravoire et Dehaze, a family business and hitherto market-leaders in the manufacture of toilet paper. But losses mount when an American paper-product giant markets a superior brand, forcing the French company to urgently review its marketing strategy.

In this speech Benoît addresses his sales force. The cut-and-thrust of the business world is his life's blood. This is a sales pitch for his ideas, a rallying cry before battle. Look how everything is described in the terminology of the battlefield. The competitor is 'the enemy', Benoît's new marketing strategy, 'the assault'. Lengthy unpunctuated sentences give it an oratorical drive. It is almost messianic in its fervour. We might be selling toilet paper but this is Agincourt. Benoît is commander of his troops, inspiring, commanding, determined and confident. 'A few organisational changes' is business-speak for 'root and branch'. Executive action is skimpily dressed as consultation. One can't help feeling by the end that he deserves a round of applause.

Moss and Heather is the brand name of the company's forthcoming new product by the way, designed to increase the consumer's lavatorial pleasures and sharpen the company's competitive edge.

---

**Benoît** I'm here to tell you where we are and where we're going at the moment we're at rock bottom and we'll stay there for a little while longer bracing ourselves for the assault and then we're going to leap forward and those of you who don't rise to the challenge will soon find you don't belong here any more this isn't a threat it's a statement of fact I know you can all make it the question is do you want to? With our new product due for launch early next year we shall not only recapture all the ground we have ceded to the enemy but we shall also push back the very limits of the market if you say to me I'm a dreamer then I'll answer yes I am a dreamer it has always been dreamers who have smashed apparently insuperable obstacles there have been rumblings among you because I have more than doubled expenditure yes I have and I did so in order to sharpen our competitive edge on the other hand there are expenses which you may think are unavoidable which I shall do away with cutbacks will be drastic in all departments one thing is finished for certain and I'm not asking you this I'm telling you all the squabbling all the bickering in back rooms no longer has any place in the firm for the simple reason that we need all our time and energy to accomplish the task at hand finally I am injecting some new blood into the business together with a few organisational changes Yves Battistini fresh from Proctor and Gamble will start up a department of marketing research Jean-Baptiste Peyre until now product manager at Johnson's Wax will become product group manager Battistini Peyre and Claude Dutôt will form the pillars of our marketing department André Saillant in the newly created position of controller will re-energise our entire financial and administrative structures I have promoted one of you Grangier to the key position of factory manager from now on purchasing shall report to the factory and henceforth Madame Bachevski will be accountable to Grangier one final word in any business what really makes the difference is the people which is why the personnel department is now entrusted to my brother Olivier he will be able to tend to it exclusively now that he is relieved of responsibility for production all that remains is for me to thank you.

# Speed-the-Plow *by David Mamet*

**Speed-the-Plow** is a satirical comedy set in the fawning empire of Tinseltown. Bobby Gould is around forty. He is the newly promoted head of film production for a big Hollywood studio. Suddenly he's a big player with a direct line to the head of the studio – a mover and a shaker. He is scheming, unprincipled, foul-mouthed, ambitious, sexist and manipulative. An 'old whore' and proud of it. 'He takes his coffee like his movies – nothing in it.'

A colleague, Charlie Fox, has just brought him a package for a big commercial blockbuster. It has everything going for it – sex, titillation, violence, and it also has a big star in tow. Gould smells money.

But before heading off for a power lunch to celebrate he talks to Karen, a gorgeous temp in his office. She is half his age and Fox has bet him a hundred bucks that he can't get her into bed! When she asks if the proposed movie will be 'a good film' Gould is floored by the naivety of the question. Does he know what a good film is? As far as he's concerned it's 'Never mind the quality, how much money will it make?' But that's not an answer for a beautiful, idealistic woman – especially if you want to win a bet!

He begins with flattery, stalling for time as he tries to frame an answer that will show him in a good light. His tack is to present himself as an honest businessman, doing his best but faced with practical reality. He grows more expansive. He shifts the question from the aesthetic qualities of the film to business. Business not art is his territory. His thought processes become more coherent. He has to make tough decisions. Loyalty is what matters. People are what matter. He almost believes it. Sincerity oozes from every pore. He is 'Mr Big', captain of the ship, a kindly teacher, a business guru, schooling a grateful disciple on how business is done.

But remember that however Gould presents himself, these are the first steps in a mating dance. If we hadn't seen a very different man in earlier scenes, it would be a convincing performance!

---

81

**Gould** You ask me, is it a good film? Well, it's a commodity. And I admire you for not being ashamed to ask the question. Yes, it's a good question, and I don't *know* if it is a good film. 'What about Art?' I'm no artist. Never said I was, and nobody who sits in this chair can be. I'm a businessman. 'Can't we try to make good films?' Yes. We try. I'm going to try to make a good film of this prison film. The question: Is there such a thing as a good film which loses money? In general, of course. But, really, not. For *me*, 'cause if the films I make lose money, then I'm back on the streets with a sweet and silly smile on my face, they lost money 'cause nobody saw them, it's my fault. A tree fell in the forest, what did I accomplish? Yes. You *see*? There is a way things are. Some people are elected, try to change the world, this job is not that job. Somebody, somebody . . . in this job, in the job I have, somebody is always trying to 'promote' you: to use *something*, some 'hook' to get you to do something in their own best interest. You follow me? 'Cause this *desk* is a position to *advance*, y'understand? It's a *platform* to *aid*, to push someone along. But I Can't *Do* It. Why? That's not my business. My business is to make decisions for the studio. Means I have to be *blunt*, to say 'no', much, most of the time, that's my job. And I think it's a *good* job: 'cause it's a job of *responsibility*. Pressure, many rewards. *One* of them, one time in a billion years, someone was loyal to me, and I'm talking about Charlie Fox, stuck *with* me, comes in here, let's face it, does a favour for me . . . he could of took the script across the street, no, but he came to me, now – I can throw in with him and we rise together. That's what the job is. It's a job, all the bullshit aside, deals with *people*. (*He hunts on his desk, picks up a copy of the book he was reading from earlier.*) Look here. Agent gives his client's book to Ross: 'The Bridge or, Radiation and the Half-Life of Society': Now, *who* is Mister Ross, now . . .? He is the Head of the Studio. And he has a button on my console. That's right. Author's agent gave this book to Ross. A novel. Written by a Very Famous Eastern Writer. What's this book about? 'The End of the World.' Great. Now: Ross, no dummy, says, of course, he'll read the book. Gives *me* the book to read, so when he tells the author 'how he loved the book but it won't make a movie', he can say something intelligent about it. You get it? This, in the business, is called 'a courtesy read'. No one has any intention of making the book, but we read it, as a courtesy. Does this mean that we're depraved? No. It's just business . . . how business is done, you see?

# Rat in the Skull *by Ron Hutchinson*

Detective Inspector Nelson is an officer in the Royal Ulster Constabulary. He is an Orangeman in his forties. He has been recalled from holiday to interrogate Michael Patrick de Valera Demon Bomber Roche who has been pulled in for questioning under the Prevention of Terrorism Act. On the face of it it's 'bang to rights'. Explosives have been found under Roche's bed. But an 'overenthusiastic' arrest has left Roche looking as if he's been in a traffic accident. Now careers are on the line. Prospects of 'The Met' closing a two-year investigation are beginning to crumble. Nelson is the 'heavy RUC gun' shipped in to secure a conviction. The two men confront each other for the first time in an interrogation room at London's Paddington Green police station. Roche refuses to speak to the Royal 'Ugly' Constabulary (as he describes them). Nelson is 'pissed off' at having his leave wrecked and is determined to break him.

Nelson is a 'specialist' with a track record of 'turning hard cases a hundred and eighty'. He's tough and intelligent. A passionate Loyalist. He knows the Republican mentality. He knows instinctively that he and Roche are on opposite sides of the same brutal coin and that he will need all his skill to prise open the clam; 'get in behind his eyeballs', 'make him bite'. This is a confrontation of equals. The words Roche does not speak Nelson puts into his mouth. It is a practised performance. He is by turns, mercurial, casual, calculating, insulting, perplexed, sarcastic and friendly. He knows which buttons to push, and he pushes them all. He uses language like a scalpel, each cut careful, swift and calculated. One minute he is the 'orange gorilla', the archetypal bully boy cop, threatening and vicious, the next he is all urbanity, offering Roche a cup of tea.

But there is much more to this speech than the usual 'copper and con' dynamic. Ron Hutchinson describes his play as 'Yours truly arguing with himself – trying to square his Northern Irish Protestant heritage with a deeper sense of Irishness, setting his head against his heart, trying to find a position.' A good note. This is Nelson's internal discourse too.

*The lights switch up on* **Roche,** *waiting for the interrogation.*

**Naylor** *sits as* **Nelson** *takes his time surveying* **Roche.**

**Nelson** Pulled back from leave, for this. For you.

Why bother, I said? Your man has coughed fifteen pages, you have his name on it. He'll go back on it, sure, shout rape and blue murder when the trial date's fixed, how they booted it out of him. But that won't wash – (*Flipping through the file.*) A medical check after every interview, not a mark on you. Though that won't stop you trying. Will it? (*Waiting.*) And there he'll sit, the Human Clam. Tight as the fundament of the shark at several atmospheres. Saying nothing, least of all to a gorilla from the RUC.

(*At* **Naylor.**) What did he say when they told him I was flying in? Nothing doing? The only way he'll speak to an RUC man is through a medium? Give him two thousand foot of wire and a ton of high explosive, he might say yes?

(*Back towards* **Roche.**) And you know and I know, between you and me and the cell door, there's no real point to me digging into you about events and characters back home, is there?

These boys aren't going to let you home in a hurry. They pulled you in, they're going to keep you. Whatever you might have been up to back in Belfast, it's more important that you get done for breaking a few shop windows in Oxford Street or disturbing the traffic in Horse Guards Parade.

Name of the game. *Nom de jouer.*

So I've had my leave wrecked for bugger all and you're missing out on shuteye for likewise. You'll just sit there, playing with your papist prick –

(*Waiting.*) Sorry. Crude, that. The kind of thing you'd expect from a cop. But I'm not here as a cop, am I? Because you said you wouldn't see one – not from back home anyway. So if I'm here at all, I'll just be another fella from the quare old place, God love it, looking for a wee bit of crack with a fellow countryman –

(*As if puzzled, to* **Naylor**.) But now we have a problem. Your man here denies the existence – note – the existence, not just the right to exist but the established fact, the stub-your-toe-on-the-concrete reality that there is such a place as –

Holey Moley – we can't even agree on a name for what we're fighting about. Ulster? The Six Counties? The North-East? The Bloody North? (*Shrugs*.) Forget that for now, let's just say I'm another brand of Irishman.

And then again – how could a mongrel dog like me ever claim that proud name, answering in a confusing sort of way to being half of everything and nothing much of anything – Scots, Irish, Irish Scots, but ever just the one and certain fact, one thing for sure in the entire bloody boiling – no way straight Irish on the rocks? (*A sigh*.) So I'm here as a copper after all. We can hang on to that.

(*Back to* **Roche**.) I'm a cop and you're a poor unfortunate sod found with enough how's-your-father under your bunk to send you into orbit if you smoked in bed.

Copper and con. (*Slaps his forehead*.) Jumping Jehoshaphat – that doesn't work either, does it? Because there's a war on and I'm a collaborator with the Army of Occupation – a traitor working for the Brits in a colonial war, so the normal rules don't apply. (*Relaxing*.) So why don't we say, this is just fellas, from somewhere around the same neck of the woods, having a wee chat about nothing in particular. (*Beat*.) Except the one fella isn't going to say a word to the other because the one fella says the only time he's pleased at the sight of an RUC man is when he's in that pine box and his cap neatly on top of it and a lot of people walking behind it crying their eyes out and I've seen that many a time the past few years, too many –

(*Alert, waiting for a response*.) Were you going to say something? You've followed a lifetime of coffins down your narrow streets and all?

I'm sure you have. So that's something we have in common. But not enough for the purposes of conversation, polite or otherwise, I see. Your lips are sealed.

(*Closer to* **Roche**.) I'm going to break you, son. Come the end of the day I'll have you because I am one pissed-off cop who's had his leave wrecked for you and I will get inside you, pal, I will get behind your eyeballs and your lungs, I will wear your ears and nipples. I will feel your swinging, banging balls between my legs and I will hear you say –

(*Stopping suddenly, a smile to* **Naylor**.) I wouldn't mind a cup of tea. Two. One for me and one for Roche here.

# They Are Dying Out *by Peter Handke*

This play is an almost Brechtian satire on capitalist society
and big business – Brechtian in as much as the suffering of
Handke's characters often appears more intellectual and
literary than felt.

At its centre is the struggle of Hermann Quitt, a wealthy
corporate mogul, to assert his individuality in the face of all
the demands of his social role and corporate position. Quitt
is a sad, lonely man in an empty marriage, a tragic figure
who reaches out to make contact with feelings that have
been long buried. The emotional has been wholly
subsumed by the rational. He feels 'caught inside his skin'
and longs for spontaneity, originality, escape. 'I lead a
businessman's life as camouflage' he says. He has lost the
broader picture of his life in the detail of everyday existence.

To comfort him, his servant Hans reads an extract from
the nineteenth-century writer, Adalbert Stifter, and it is to
this that he responds.

The reading is about freedom, the beauty of nature and
the nobility of the human spirit. It touches some well-
spring of longing in Quitt for another way of being and
suddenly the prospect of throwing everything in the air,
making a new start, sloughing off the old order becomes a
real possibility. Look how the speech gains momentum and
energy and how Quitt becomes more gleeful and engaged as
the idea takes root. It must build to its almost biblical
climax with the old order being swept away and real
thunder rending the air.

As soon as his servant leaves Quitt will drum his fists on
his chest and emit Tarzan-like screams in an atavistic
expression of his bid for freedom. This is what the speech is
building to.

———————————

**Quitt** How nice that this armchair has a headrest. (*Pause.*) How much time has passed since then! In those days, in the nineteenth century, even if you didn't have some feeling for the world, there at least existed a memory of a universal feeling, and a yearning. That is why you could replay the feeling and replay it for the others as in this story. And because you could replay the feeling as seriously and patiently and conscientiously as a restorer – Adalbert Stifter after all was a restorer – that feeling was really produced, perhaps. In any event, people believed that what was being played there existed, or at least that it was possible. All I actually do is quote; everything that is meant to be serious immediately becomes a joke with me, genuine signs of life of my own slip out of me purely by accident, and they only exist at the moment when they slip out. Afterwards then they are – well – where you once used to see the whole, I see nothing but particulars now. Hey, you with your ingrown earlobes. It suddenly slips out of me, and, instead of speaking to someone I notice, I step on his heels so that his shoe comes off. I would so like to be full of pathos! Von Wullnow bathing in the nude with a couple of women at sunrise bawled nothing but old college songs in the water – that's what's left of him. What slips out of me is only the raw sewage of previous centuries. I lead a businessman's life as camouflage. I go to the telephone as soon as it rings. I talk faster if the door behind me is held open. We fix our prices and faithfully stick to our agreements. Suddenly it occurs to me that I am playing something that doesn't even exist, and that's the difference. That's the despair of it! Do you know what I'm going to do? I won't stick to our arrangement. I'm going to ruin their prices and them with it. I'm going to employ my old-fashioned sense of self as a means of production. I haven't had anything of myself as yet, Hans. And they are going to cool their hot little heads with their clammy hands, and their heads will grow cold as well. It will be a tragedy. A tragedy of business life, and I will be the survivor. And the investment in the business will be me, just me alone. I will slip out of myself and the raw sewage will sweep them away. There will be lightning and thunder, and the idea will become flesh.

*There is thunder.*

# Eleven Vests *by Edward Bond*

This is a play for three actors in seven scenes. It is very loosely based on the real-life murder of secondary school headmaster, Philip Lawrence, in a West London school in the 1990s.

The Head's age is not specified but he is not young.

In the first scene he accuses a student of vandalising a school book. Pompous, inept, manipulative and out of touch, he pulls every teacher's cliché out of the hat to persuade the student to acknowledge what he has done. But to no avail. See how he changes tack when each approach fails and how he uses language the student could not possibly identify with; how he threatens, cajoles, disparages, flatters, appeals to the student's 'better nature', and even shares confidences to achieve the desired effect. His efforts only serve to alienate and underline his lack of understanding at the disaffection that engenders such wanton destruction.

As his frustration and impotence mount, he becomes more ludicrous, banging his head ineffectually against the brick wall of the student's rebellious silences. It is a power struggle that he cannot win. His patronising authority is a thin veneer for his contempt for the student and the unbridgeable gap between their life-styles and value systems. Finally, running out of steam and arguments, he is forced into ignominious retreat.

The seeds of his own murder are already planted. In the writer's own words, '. . . in one shape or another, violence always returns to unleash its wrath on the ignorance of the society that creates it. And we are an ignorant society.'

---

*The* **Head** *questions the* **Student**.

**Head** Why? D'you know why? What did you gain by it? Answer me. Do you deny it's your handiwork? Well? I didn't see you do it. No one did. I accuse you because I know none of my other pupils would do it. It has your trademark all over it. And you did it on your own. You couldn't involve anyone else. The others wouldn't be so stupid. Aren't you going to speak? I shall take your silence as a confession of guilt. Well? Thank you for not wasting my time with fatuous denials. At least you spare me that. Not that you lack the effrontery to deny it and let the blame fall on some innocent person. A selfish disregard for the well-being of others. Only you're too clever to try. Yes that made you look at me! You know you wouldn't get away with it. Why did you do it? I'd like an explanation – or at least an excuse. Take your time. I can wait.

*He takes out a book with slashed pages.*

Destruction for destruction's sake. Take it. Are you ashamed to hold it in your hands?

*The* **Head** *tries to give the* **Student** *the book. The* **Student** *refuses it. The* **Head** *wedges a corner of the book in the* **Student***'s pocket and steps back. The book falls to the ground.*

**Head** D'you want to be expelled? Don't look out of the window when I talk to you. Don't look on the ground. I suppose you think this silence makes you tough? You don't have to conform because you're special? Too good for us! You're not. I've seen them standing where you are – the no-hopers, the non-achievers. I see you five years from now. I read you like this book – only it makes more sense than you do even in the dilapidated state you've reduced it to. Some of our young people respect books. They want to learn. Now I shall have to lock the library room when it's unattended. Would-be readers will have to come to my secretary for the key. So everyone is punished because of you. You're not stepping out of this room till you say something. D'you think I like questioning you? Exercising my power? I have better things to waste my time on. I get no satisfaction from knocking my head on a brick wall. I do it so that you can't tell yourself you had no chance. You're not going to deceive yourself on that! You're given every chance. Are you going to speak? I try to help you because you can't help yourself. Pick up the book and tell me why you vandalised it. Then we'll forget about it. I don't have to report it to the governors. We'll throw it in the bin and you can go back to your class. My secretary will find out what it cost. You will pay for it in instalments. We'll set a weekly sum you can afford. Our parents have to work to buy books for the school. I suppose that doesn't concern you? You won't get a job – you won't try – so you'll never be asked to pay for anything. Pick it up. It makes no difference to me what you do. It make a great deal of difference to me when school property is destroyed. I did concern myself with you once. When you entered this school with your intake I had hopes for all of you. I didn't make the world what it is. I hoped I could help you and the others to survive in it. I even hoped that when the time came for you to leave some of you would go out and make it a better place. That's why I became a teacher. There! – I've confessed something to you about my life. Can't you confess about a *book*? Just say you regret what you've done. You don't even have to mean it. Just make the gesture to what decent civilised people do. Then we have a foundation to build a relationship on. It's only a book. You're worth more than a book. Tell me something: don't you want to be happy? I don't think you do. It's too simple. You don't know why you destroyed the book. You don't know why you do anything. It's not just me you can't talk to. You can't talk to yourself. That's why you'll destroy yourself. If this were a story you'd end up running the school library. Life isn't like that. It's like this book. I can't spare you any more time. I have things to attend to. Other pupils have needs. I shall write to your parents. If you commit any further nuisance you will be expelled. This is the final warning. I shall have to put you down as one of my failures. Please close the door as you go.

*The* **Head** *watches the* **Student** *go and then picks up the book and goes in the opposite direction.*

# Sore Throats *by Howard Brenton*

This is a drama about the breakdown of a marriage and its aftermath. The play shifts between naturalistic exchanges and counterpointing bursts of soliloquy that reveal unspoken thoughts and feelings. Jack is aged forty-five, a police chief inspector and a wife beater. He has subjected his wife, Judy, to countless savage attacks over more than twenty years of marriage. He is a selfish, sexist bully with a short, unpredictable fuse.

Jack has left Judy for Celia with whom he is hopelessly obsessed. Jack and Judy are about to divorce. The split has been painful and destructive. Literally blood on the carpet. Jack has come to Judy's flat to claim his share of their house – money he relinquished in an ill-judged fit of guilty conscience. Now he needs it to start a new life with Celia in Canada. He rightly suspects that Judy won't play ball.

The monologue begins with Jack telling Judy how Celia makes him feel. He is impervious to Judy's pain, presenting himself as a sensitive man, a man in love. But the internal dialogue we hear tells another story. Look at Howard Brenton's stage directions. There are three asides – cues to change gear from naturalism to soliloquy. He gives us a couple of helpful notes on this. 'Imagine Judy and Jack . . . with their minds splitting open, their innermost half-thoughts and feelings pulled out of them like ticker-tape or ragged banners, from their heads . . .'

Jack's secret thoughts are expressed in a self-obsessed stream of consciousness – the equivalent of a dirty magazine hidden under the mattress. You'll see there is never a mention of sharing, taking responsibility. It's all selfish, greedy, sexual need. Rhetorical question tumbles over rhetorical question as he justifies following his penis where it leads. After all, doesn't he want what we all want? Isn't he entitled to freedom, a bit of love?

But Jack can't follow his dream without half the money from the house. Since he arrived he has been gearing up to ask for it, and when Judy refuses he predictably gives her a terrible beating until she gives him what he wants.

**Jack** When I first saw her. Celia. You know – naked, I cried. I couldn't stop crying. (*Looking at his hands.*) I was helpless, my hands. I faltered. Felt ashamed. I. So real, she was the real world. The dignity, the – after so long. I'd forgotten, perhaps I'd never known. How beautiful we are. How simple.

(*Aside.*) After all, we all want a good fuck! On the whole! In one hole or another!

*He scoffs.*

(*Aside.*) Human beings. Want to get up each other. Be got up by each other. That's life. Slosh about, have a heavy breathe. And burst, all over.

So why all the bitterness, why all the agony? When all you want is a bit of tenderness, a bit of tender – good time. Get warm, get inflamed. Stretched. So why this third world war, in your living room, in your bathroom in your bedroom, about who fucks who?

*He scoffs.*

(*Aside.*) And why, in marriage, when all you want is – comfort, just to get your cock and all the works behind, a bit comfortable – do you end up talking about the insulation in the loft all the time? The cost of sheets! Woodworm in the floorboards! The cost of kiddies' shoes! Domestic Savings Policy!

I mean not even a pig should be asked to fuck a Trustees Savings Bank Account!

In the last stages of my divorce, I had a bit of a fantasy. One night, driven mad by the mill of marriage and sex, I saw myself discovered by a fellow police officer, outside a Trustees Savings Bank, my trousers and my Y-fronts down, my bum exposed to the night air and the fingers of passing drunks – with my cock jammed in a twenty-four-hour cash dispensing machine.

Trying to reconcile money and sex.

You've got to be free. Or you've got to feel free. That you do things freely. Or one thing, the best thing. Love.

Even if you're a policeman, you've got to feel that!

'Else, what is there?

# Leonardo's Last Supper *by Peter Barnes*

This is a one-act comedy set in an undertaker's in medieval France. Lasca is a heavy, vulgar, opportunistic, self-interested, middle-aged man with few morals. He's a wheeler-dealer with an eye to every main chance. He's in exile from his native Florence (no Italian accents please) and inheritor of his father's undertaking business – the Amboise Charnel House.

Leonardo da Vinci is dead and it has fallen to Lasca, a fellow Florentine, to take care of the funeral arrangements. There's a small fortune to be made. Grand masses, low masses and the lavish funeral itself. This could buy him out of all sorts of difficulties. But his glee is short-lived as the great man rises from his winding sheet alive and kicking. The unappetising apparition of the rascally Lasca convinces Leonardo that he must be in Hell. He seeks proof positive of his vitality by demanding talk of his beloved Florence so he can judge whether Lasca knows 'the shape and feel of being alive'. Lasca is only too happy to oblige. He and his family talk of little else.

In this speech Lasca describes 'the good old days' of the plague year, 1494. It was a great year for Lasca and his family. With so many dead, business was booming and there were great opportunities to diversify. Lasca spotted a gap in the market, developing his own innovative and lucrative remedies against the plague. He describes his initiatives with entrepreneurial zeal and his fall, with wounded spleen.

Peter Barnes has developed a unique vernacular for this little play. It tastes of the period yet still delivers a contemporary punch. As for how to play the lines, I can do no better than quote Peter Barnes himself . . . 'the meaning is in the lines, not between them. Absolute precision is essential; the words must be hit dead centre. No "fluting", with the actor enjoying the sound of the words rather than their meaning. Precision and speed. Not necessarily in the delivery of the lines, but speed of thought and reaction . . .'

**Lasca** The public always looks f' something new and fresh. I gave it to 'em, thanks in part to your famous method, Signor da Vinci. You said to look to facts as they are and not to rank superstition and magic, 'Swhat I did. I used me eyes and ears. In time o' pestilence I noted that tomturd men and privy cleaners never fell sick. They were protected by the stench o' their work. The stink clinging to their persons protected 'em from the plague. I wasn't the only sharper who noted it. At the height of the pestilence crowds used to stand in front o' private privies sniffing up the smells. (*Sniffs loudly.*) Privy owners soon got to charging 'em twenty-five denari an hour for the privilege. I set out to manufacture medicinal smells. I bottled farts. We had a team o' wind-breakers, Signor. I fed 'em on radishes and beans. When they were in the producing way they'd lift up their skirts, drop their breeches and stick a green bottle up their arse. *Bang.* And we had a little o' that most healing physic, 'Lasca's Sweet Morning Wind'. Price one florin; three denari back on all empties. But wind's difficult to bottle. A couple o' sniffs and 'tis gone. Customers wanted something more solid. So next I bottled shit. Pilgrim's salve, 100 per cent proof. 'Lasca's Excremental Goodness' came in three sizes. 'Lady's Own' was a tiny bottle most beautifully engraved with signs o' the zodiac and attached to a gold necklace. 'Man Size' was flat and decorated with the figure o' Hercules strangling a lion; it sold at six florins. Our 'Jumbo Family jar' cost all o' ten florins, but it lasted weeks. Signor, I'd discovered the secret o' wealth. I o'ertopped those learned alchemists. They only turned *lead* into gold. We lived high, like true princes o' the Church. I was a mighty meat-eater then: bloodmeat makes the sinews supple. Boiled owl and roasted boar with sweet sauce and pine kernels; bear hams and baked porpentine. I became particular partial to venison – fat and full o' blood. All washed down with black Marino wine. (*Burps loudly.*) Jesus, how we lived. Then I was forced to join the Apothecaries' Guild, with their gut and garbage rules for honest trading. *Sallow pates!* They couldn't see honesty's one thing and trading's something else again. The moment I put 'Lasca's Excremental Goodness' on the market out came their rules and regulations. They laid down the price for shit at sixty florins a ton.

Can you credit it, Signor? Sixty florins! I told them it was too low. I could get 150 florins without strain. Then they sent this weasel-eyed Inspector o' Turds round sniffing and spying. Had me up in front o' a full Guild Court accused o' overcharging and watering down my merchandise. I had nothing to hide. But they stopped their ears and found me guilty. 'Twas envy, black cancerous envy. I was fined 5,000 florins and no time to pay. We caught a disease worse than the Black Death itself – poverty.

# Don Juan on Trial *by Eric-Emmanuel Schmitt*

Don Juan is no longer young but he still has his legendary charisma and a silver tongue that flatters and beguiles.

When the Don arrives at the Duchess de Vaubricourt's crumbling château, he thinks he has been invited to a ball, but the Duchess has something very different in store for him. She has also summoned four other women who, like her, have been seduced and abandoned by Don Juan. They have come to judge and condemn him for the damage he has done to them. His punishment (for his guilt is a foregone conclusion) is to marry Angelique, the Duchess's twenty-year-old niece, another of his innocent victims, whose brother he has killed in a duel. His penance is to remain faithful to her (a new experience for Don Juan) or be incarcerated in the Bastille. To everyone's surprise Don Juan accepts his punishment without argument. It is not until the end of the play that we understand why.

In this scene he is alone with the infatuated Angelique. He has told her he doesn't love her but has been blackmailed into marriage by the Duchess. Angelique is horrified and asks him what he is looking for in life.

In this speech he sets out his philosophy. It is a sensual panegyric to pleasure. No holds barred. Don Juan is all appetite. Sex is his enthusiasm, the force that drives him. The case he makes for the pursuit of pleasure, though flawed and amoral, should be totally compelling. We must have no difficulty in understanding why his victims, however badly treated, remain in thrall.

Ironically it is not a woman, but the sacrifice and devotion of another man, that makes Don Juan reassess his values, begin to understand the true nature of love and seek a new way of being.

---

**Don Juan** Why should you imagine I'm looking for anything? I don't look. I take, I pluck the apples from the bough and crunch them with my teeth. And then, when I'm hungry, I grab some more. That's hardly a quest, is it? Hardly a search. Merely appetite. My mouth wants to savour every kind of fruit. Every kind of mouth. Fat ones, juicy ones, tender ones, and hard ones, closed, open, the narrow mouth of the prude, the sunken lips of the sensualist, the astonished pout of the schoolgirl, I want them all. Men, my love, men envy me, because I do what they wouldn't dare to do – and women resent me because I give pleasure to all of them. All of them. You're all afraid of pleasure and you're right to be. Only the strong know how to channel it. Imagine if the edict went out to the whole world: 'Put down your pickaxes, and your needles and thread. Our new currency is pleasure. Take some, take lots, here, now, without shame.' What'd happen? No one would be there to work, to sweat, to fight. Idle men, devoted entirely to pleasure. No children would be legitimate or illegitimate – just a vast babble of brats with thirty-six mothers, and 120 fathers. No more property, or inheritance or blood privileges, because blood would be generally spread about, like sperm, flowing everywhere. Life would be one big happy bordello. With nothing but whores – no customers, and no pimps. Can you imagine the wonderful unholy mess? What would happen to trade, industry, families, fortune. No more money, no more poverty, because pleasure would be the only wealth, and in that regard we are all equally gifted. So tell me things I've heard a thousand times, this nonsense about quests, searches. One only seeks what one has not found. Only the frustrated and the hopeless search – the happy man doesn't bother. I've never had to look far for pleasure, and that's all I've ever wished for.

# Jesus Hopped the 'A' Train
## *by Stephen Adly Guirgis*

This is a hard-hitting drama about the quest for morality and grace in the New York City criminal justice system. The play takes place largely in the yard of a special twenty-three-hour lock-down wing of protective custody on Rikers Island – a place where brutality and racism are the order of the day.

Lucius Jenkins is a notorious inmate – a psychotic, drug-abusing serial killer from the black underclass who is facing the death sentence. He is the product of an abusive and violated childhood in the ghetto. He is middle-aged, compelling and keeps himself fit with vigorous workouts in the prison yard. He enjoys his 'Superstar' status in the prison. While behind bars Lucius has found God through a 'road to Damascus' conversion and purveys his beliefs to warder and prisoner alike with the 'door-stepping' fervour of the convert.

In this speech, Lucius is talking to a new inmate, Angel Cruz, an impressionable young Puerto Rican who is awaiting trial for murder of born-again Reverend Kim. They occupy adjacent cages in the yard. Angel is coping badly with prison life and Lucius has been at pains to gain his trust. At this point, Angel has accepted a cigarette from Lucius and is beginning to open up. This gives Lucius the opportunity to preach his message.

In spite of the shocking content of Lucius's story, he might be describing a walk in the park. Remember that this is just the stuff of Lucius's life – its impact will be diminished if you deliver it in any other way. Lucius believes that somehow faith has automatically absolved him of these brutal crimes. God has become both an addiction and a solution – a Band-Aid for his pain and an emotional escape route from the harsh prison regime. His agenda here is to sell the magic cure to Angel.

Look at the messianic rhetoric at the end of the speech. Religion has let the sun into Lucius's life and given him a strategy for survival in the bleakest places.

**Lucius** OK, so, lissen careful: there I was, Miami Beach. Paradise, right? Little apartment complex they got over there, second floor, view of the ocean, the ladies, everything . . . The ladies down there in Miami, Angel? Like nobody's business, brother – awesome, incredible . . . Rent was cheap – didn't pay but four hundred bucks a month on that little place . . . Did I mention it had a little terrace? Well, it did. Never went out on it . . . Cocaine in Miami? Plentiful, jack. Extremely plentiful. And cheap. Real cheap. Dirt cheap. For all intents and purposes, the shit was free. Pardon my language, but, that's what cocaine is. Shit . . . Horseshit . . . Anyway – Oh! and Qualudes? Them, little 714s? Like takin' aspirin, baby. Take two, call me late for dinner . . . Heroin, Dilaudid? Juss pick up the phone! Thirty minutes, home delivery! . . . Hated the sun though, hated it . . . I'm not talkin' 'bout 'Gee, I wish it wasn't so sunny', I'm talkin' Hate . . . Pathological Dracula Shit . . . Deep . . . Came a time, I stopped goin' in ta work if it was too sunny. Usedta call in sick, order a pizza and a twelve-pack. Pizza and a twelve-pack for 8.50, how ya gonna beat that?! Delivery boy, he was all right, little Ecuadorean kid, usedta pick me up a little somethin' on the way, a nice bag, coupla pornos, whatever I wanted, usedta blow a little smoke wit him, he'd leave happy. Nice little system. One day, he stopped by . . . I killed him. Killed him with a cowboy boot . . . I mean, I was wearin' the boot at the time, thass how I killed him . . . After I killed him, I didn't know what ta do so I chopped him up, threw him, in the dumpster, right next door. Next door! Can ya imagine that? . . . And ya know what happened? . . . Nuthin' . . . Not a damn thing . . . Kept waitin' for the sirens, they never came . . . So I called up the pizza shop, toal 'em: 'I never got my pizza.' You know what they did? . . . They sent me another one. For free . . . Now, to me, that's a peculiar turn of events, doncha think? . . . Unnatural . . . I'll tell ya why I killed him . . . I killed him 'cuz he left the door open, said the place stunk, needed some air. But when the air came in . . . the sun came with it . . . Now . . . I think, I think that was a very unusual thing for me to do, killing that boy, don't you? . . . Highly unusual . . . And . . . Nuthin' happened! Nuthin' . . . One day, I finally got up the gumption to leave Miami, but, by then,

I had killed five people . . . Five . . . Killed three more up north, over here, but they was all white. Funny how people start payin' attention when white people start droppin' . . . And all a this, 'cuz I hated the sun . . . My enemy. The sun . . . I had everything in the world down there but I didn't have nuthin'. Now I got nuthin' but I got everythin'. I love the sun now. Love it . . . Before? Hate. Now? Love . . . Dass a conundrum, Kimosabee . . . When ya get back to your cell? Doan' lie down . . . When ya can't do nuthin' else except lie down? Then ya gonna lie down and dig on what I juss toal' ya . . . reflect . . . Every hour, I'm a bang on my wall three times, let ya remember you ain't alone, OK?

# Fashion *by Doug Lucie*

The relationship between politics and the advertising industry is the theme of Doug Lucie's acerbic drama set in the run-up to a general election at the height of the Thatcher era.

Howard Lipton is middle-aged, and upper-crust. He has several company directorships, a thriving family business and houses on three continents. He is an unreconstructed 'gentleman', 'born to rule' Tory of 'the public school tendency' with a stronger sense of public service than his public persona indicates. His dialogue throughout the play is littered with expressions like 'the good lady wife' and 'our dusky chum' which gives you a clue to his character. He is spearheading a presentation for the forthcoming election campaign.

He has brought Gillian Huntley, a self-seeking prospective parliamentary candidate, to learn TV presentation skills at the offices of Cash Creative Consultancy. Prior to this he has rather unwisely 'shafted her' in her hotel bedroom after an over-indulgent lunch.

Howard has presented himself as something of a Vicar of Bray – adjusting his allegiances as required. In reality his agenda is to use Gillian to undermine Thatcher's leadership in favour of a more moderate successor. But things don't go quite as planned. During the mock interview Gillian Huntley is revealed as a prejudiced authoritarian who makes Margaret Thatcher look like a 'lefty'. Howard is horrified!

His response is furious but in control. ('I have seen the future,' he says after she has gone, 'and it freezes my water.')

Obey the writer's instructions and you will find the pace and measure of this speech. He delivers a series of well-aimed blows at the heart of all Gillian stands for. He impugns her mental health, savages her idol Mrs Thatcher, treats her like a spoilt child and finally relegates her to rural obscurity out of harm's way. If Gillian were a butterfly he would be carefully, lethally pulling off wings and legs. This is slow, calculated, public humiliation, which the ruthless Gillian will not forget.

---

**Howard** I mean, speaking as a fellow Briton, I get the impression that you feel we're just not good enough. We fail to measure up to some abstract standard you have for . . . attitude, behaviour. We're just not good enough, and you're jolly well going to do something about it! (*He smiles. Beat.*) Forgive me, but that is the most preposterous, dangerous nonsense it has ever been my misfortune to hear. I have been in politics all my adult life. I have known people who came into politics to further their business careers, to boost their egos, to fill an otherwise dull life, to fulfil the family tradition. I have even known people come into politics because they believe they have something useful to offer the nation. But I have never known anybody come into politics because they despise their country and wish to exorcise their fear and loathing with a good dose of corrective medicine. That is not political drive. That is psychological disorder. (*Beat.*) Please don't make the mistake of thinking that we want an army of steel-jawed, flaxen-haired warriors against all things decadent. Our leader is a one-off. She can't go on for ever. She is useful in the short term for enabling us to do what we do best: running the capitalist economy. But in the long term, she is just another servant of the Party. (*Beat.*) I just don't think we need any more like you. (*Beat.*) I'm sorry, Miss Huntley, if one day you put your little foot outside Mother and Father's ivy-covered cottage and saw lots of frightening things. I'm sorry if you didn't understand what all those horrible big grown-ups were doing, in their factories, their offices, their pubs, their bedrooms. I'm sorry they called you nasty names, and swore and didn't go to church very often; they did things Mummy and Daddy said weren't very nice. (*Beat.*) But I've got news for you. They've been doing it since the dawn of creation, and they're going to go on doing it whether you stamp your little foot and tell them to stop it or not. (*Beat.*) It's not society that has the problem, Miss Huntley. It's not society that's deviant. It's you. (*Beat.*) My advice would be to marry your farmer, produce your incredibly heavily EEC subsidised crops, have a couple of children, go to church regularly and quietly shrivel up in the peaceful English countryside. That, after all, is what it's there for.

# Never Land *by Phyllis Nagy*

Henri Joubert is a middle-aged Frenchman, who for many years has bizarrely rooted his cultural identity in England. He speaks only perfect RP and insists family and friends do likewise. His life's dream is to settle in England. He lives in a house perched in a treacherous hillside in southern France with his beautiful but alcoholic wife Anne and their disaffected daughter Elisabeth. His life has been a series of hair-brained schemes and failed initiatives. 'Stalled vocational rebirths' as his daughter cynically calls them. Only a job in the local perfumery and the indulgence of a caring employer has enabled him to hold his life and family together. At this point the dream prospect of a job managing a bookshop in Bristol has disintegrated. He has resigned his job at the perfumery, on the back of it, and he has lost everything.

Temporarily blinded by despair, Henri roams the harbour in torrential rain. He has been missing from home for over twenty-four hours. The house, as unstable as the relationships within it, rocks on its foundations while his family waits. He returns, soaked to the skin, removes his clothes with a resolution we have not seen before and goes to the sewing machine where his wife has been making him a suit – a suit that no longer has a purpose. He is stripped of everything in every sense. As he sews, he speaks as if trying to stitch his life back together.

This speech is not an explanation for absence, but a metaphor for the 'blind' chaotic journey of his life. This is a man who has reached the edge of the land and run out of options; a man who sees for the first time the lethal inevitability of the choices he has made. Never land is a place where dreams will never be realised. We are witnessing the terrible fall of the House of Joubert.

---

*A beat, before* **Henri** *disrobes completely. When he's done, he goes directly to the unfinished suit, gathers it up and takes it to* **Anne's** *sewing machine, where he begins to sew on the arms. He does all of this with an unhesitating purpose he seems to have lacked previously.*

**Henri** (*while sewing*) I was blind. I was blind and so I took a walk. I took a walk along the harbour. I took a walk along the harbour and I met a man from Derby. Derby? I said. I have never considered Derby. And you never will consider it, said he. Then the man from Derby showed me the probabilities. The man from Derby showed me the probabilities of a life beyond the harbour's horizon. Beyond the horizon to a place we are able to access only with our fear. I took a walk with this man. I took a long and treacherous walk with this man from Derby. All around the harbour. And it was dark. And it was such a clear black night sky that even if I were not blind I could not see which foot I put forward. I could not measure the progress we had made. And I said to this man from Derby: but how is it that I fear not the lack of probability? How is it that I fear not the ability to see my one foot move ahead or behind the other? And he took my hand, this man from Derby, and I trusted him immediately and his breath on the back of my neck gave me intense pleasure. This man with whom I shared the probabilities touched his soft soothing hand to my neck, this man with whom I shared such a gentle walk, leaned in so close so near to me closer I felt than any other human had and said: the menace is all around you, Henri, the menace spreads its net and it has caught you this is the probability this is the most likely scenario this is the sweet sweet sickness this is the cancer eating its stealthy way through the schoolgirl's bones this is the gas jet silently leaking overnight this is the lorry making its inexorable way towards the tricycle inching out of the driveway this is. It. And suddenly he kissed my eyes and my sight was restored. And then it rained.

*He stops sewing. He looks up to* **Anne, Elisabeth** *and* **Michael.**

**Henri** Anne. Fetch these people some towels. Can't you see they're shivering?

# Copenhagen *by Michael Frayn*

Werner Heisenberg is a German Jew; a nuclear physicist with a brilliant mind – best remembered for his 'uncertainty principle' and research into the functioning of the atom. The play happens between the 1920s (when Heisenberg and the Danish physicist Niels Bohr worked together to revolutionise atomic physics) and 1945. Bohr escaped to the US during the war while Heisenberg remained in Germany.

This complex and beautifully researched play is a fictional account of a real meeting that took place between Heisenberg and Bohr in Copenhagen when Denmark was under German occupation in 1941. (I recommend you read Michael Frayn's detailed postscripts about the play's historical and scientific background. You'll find them difficult but fascinating.)

These former friends and colleagues are now on opposite sides in the war. Why did Heisenberg go to Copenhagen? What did he want? What did they talk about?

This speech comes almost at the end of the play. Germany has been brought to its knees by Allied bombing. Heisenberg is telling Bohr how he was captured by an SS officer on his way home and narrowly escaped being shot by offering him American cigarettes. He describes the devastation of his homeland but at the heart of the speech we hear the anguished questions that have dogged him throughout the play. Would the fate of his beloved Germany have been different if he had been able to develop her nuclear capability? Is he responsible? Can we ever predict the impact of our actions? How much do decisions make themselves? How different would things be if we made *this* decision rather than *that*. The play explores these questions and the painful moral conundrum of whether it is right for a physicist to work on the practical exploitation of atomic energy for his country in wartime. The question of what happened at that meeting in Copenhagen remains, like Heisenberg's 'principle', uncertain.

––––––––––

**Heisenberg** That was the end of my war. The Allied troops were closing in; there was nothing more we could do. Elisabeth and the children had taken refuge in a village in Bavaria, so I went to see them before I was captured. I had to go by bicycle – there were no trains or road transport by that time – and I had to travel by night and sleep under a hedge by day, because all through the daylight hours the skies were full of Allied planes, scouring the roads for anything that moved. A man on a bicycle would have been the biggest target left in Germany. Three days and three nights I travelled. Out of Württemberg, down through the Swabian Jura and the first foothills of the Alps. Across my ruined homeland. Was this what I'd chosen for it? This endless rubble? This perpetual smoke in the sky? These hungry faces? Was this my doing? And all the desperate people on the roads. The most desperate of all were the SS. Bands of fanatics with nothing left to lose, roaming around shooting deserters out of hand, hanging them from roadside trees. The second night, and suddenly there it is – the terrible familiar black tunic emerging from the twilight in front of me. On his lips as I stop – the one terrible familiar word. 'Deserter,' he says. He sounds as exhausted as I am. I give him the travel order I've written for myself. But there's hardly enough light in the sky to read by, and he's too weary to bother. He begins to open his holster instead. He's going to shoot me because it's simply less labour. And suddenly I'm thinking very quickly and clearly – it's like skiing, or that night on Heligoland, or the one in Faelled Park. What comes into my mind this time is the pack of American cigarettes I've got in my pocket. And already it's in my hand – I'm holding it out to him. The most desperate solution to a problem yet. I wait while he stands there looking at it, trying to make it out, trying to think, his left hand holding my useless piece of paper, his right on the fastening of the holster. There are two simple words in large print on the pack: Lucky Strike. He closes the holster, and takes the cigarettes instead . . . It had worked, it had worked! Like all the other solutions to all the other problems. For twenty cigarettes he let me live. And on I went. Three days and three nights. Past the weeping children, the lost and hungry children, drafted to fight, then abandoned by their commanders. Past the starving slave-labourers walking home to France, to Poland, to Estonia. Through Gammertingen and Biberach and Memmingen. Mindelheim, Kaufbeuren, and Schöngau. Across my beloved homeland. My ruined and dishonoured and beloved homeland.

# Ghost from a Perfect Place *by Philip Ridley*

Travis Flood hails from the sixties 'heyday' of the East End when the streets were ruled by the likes of the Krays. In days gone by a snap of Travis's fingers meant 'kneecaps would fly'. He is a well-preserved sixty-year-old, every inch the gangster, threatening, strong and solid in appearance, black suit and hair dye to match. He makes a return journey to Bethnal Green to publicise his autobiography but comes unexpectedly face to face with his past in the shape of Rio, a tough young prostitute whom he picks up in the local graveyard. As events unfold, he discovers Rio is his daughter. She's the result of raping her fourteen-year-old mother back in 'the good old days'. He tries to leave but 'you don't mess with Rio' and she wants payment, 'service, or no service'. When he refuses to pay she fells him with a baseball bat.

In this scene we find him tied to a chair. He has been beaten and burned in a vicious revenge attack by Rio and her gang of man-hating Cheerleaders. At this point she too discovers the nature of their relationship. Shocked, she tells the Cheerleaders to leave. Father and daughter are alone. Bloodied and brutalised, physically and emotionally disempowered, there is nothing left for Travis but to tell the truth. The 'heyday' is over. He is no more menacing than an empty suit. The past is another country and there is no return. Even his book is a piece of vanity publishing.

His apology at the end of the speech should be heartfelt as he confronts the legacy of his past in his violent and degraded daughter. They have both done terrible things. In that, at least, there is a kind of bond and kinship.

In coming face to face with Rio, Travis is finally forced to come face to face with himself.

---

**Travis**  There is no fortune. There never was. I go to America with nothing. And that's how it stays. No swimming pool. No Cadillac. No speedboat. Just an endless succession of petty jobs. And always moving. And everywhere I go I change my name. Invent new stories about myself. In the end, I begin to forget who I am. Who I was. So I write a book . . . Yes! I wore a black suit! Crowds parted to let me through! A snap of my fingers meant kneecaps would fly! Yes! In a paradise called Bethnal Green they will remember, they will remember who I am . . . I have to publish the book myself. It costs me nearly everything I've got. The rest goes on a plane ticket and this suit. I'm the man with the white lily again. I come back here. Visit all my old haunts. But . . . hardly anybody remembers me. One old tramp laughs and says I look like a gangster. And that's it. Except . . . in a graveyard I meet a girl. We talk for a while. She says she's heard about me. We arrange to meet later. She gives me the address. But I arrive early. I talk to her grandmother. She tells me stories. And . . . I piece together another story. A story the grandmother's not even aware of. A story about me. Now I know who I am.

*Pause.*

And I'm sorry.

*Pause.*

# Keeping Tom Nice *by Lucy Gannon*

Tom, of the title, is a profoundly handicapped young man who is unable to communicate or do the simplest thing for himself. The play is about what looking after Tom does to his family.

Tom's father, Doug, is a well-educated man of about sixty who has retired early from a job in middle management to help wife Winnie with Tom's care. Doug's life is reduced to feeding, cleaning, lifting, and changing Tom with no respite or reward. He and Winnie have martyred themselves to Tom's care, accepting neither support nor advice but getting some dismal status from their selflessness. Both are exhausted and under enormous pressure, a predicament that is largely self-inflicted. Family tensions run high. Twenty-five years has taken its toll and Doug's frustration has spilled over into covert cruelties that have got out of hand – verbal abuse, slaps, pinches, Chinese burns. But Tom's watchful social worker, Stephen, is on to Doug's case and has told the authorities of his suspicions. Doug's image of himself as dedicated carer is cracking open. He knows his actions will be watched from now on. It will be another layer of pressure in a life that is already at breaking point. He can't trust himself with Tom any more. And he can't bear the thought of exposure.

This is the last speech in the play. Doug is talking to Tom in the garden. He drinks whisky, swigs Tom's medication and has taken an overdose of Winnie's anti-depressants. He has reached the end of a long road. It is a 'suicide note', confessional, riddled with guilt and a sense of failure but offering all the love and comfort of a father/son relationship that he has hitherto been unable to give.

There is no self-pity here, just resignation counterpointing bursts of lyricism – a blend of poetry and religious reference. Notice the clipped tones, a vestige of his former business self. There should be nothing sentimental about Doug's delivery. This is a bowing to the inevitable. An acknowledgement that his life has come to nothing. The speech should get slower and more slurred as the lethal cocktail takes effect.

---

**Doug** So. Here we are, Tom. At the end of the day. Charlotte is on the train, rushing thankfully back to her friends, and your mother is upstairs, with one of her heads, and we are here. So. Here we are. Father and son. But we're not alone, Tom. Never to be alone again if they have their way. From now on we'll know that they're there. That they know. Pushing back your sleeve and examining the flesh. Ghouls! Buggers! But the night's just as long as it ever was, and I'm still weary, and you still need to be changed, to be turned, to be fed, comforted. And I can't trust myself any more. Or her. And they can't stop me, and she won't stop me. Your nails need cutting. And, seeing the tension between us all, shimmering like heat on a long hard road, they treble it. Seeking to diminish it, they magnify it. (*Sings.*) 'My soul doth magnify the Lord.' Mine doesn't. Mine bloody doesn't. Does yours? No? It's a bugger, isn't it? We should have sat like this more often. Father and son. God, it's years since I had a skinful. Medicine to make everything better. Every little thing.

*Pours some into his whisky tumbler, a little fuddled now.*

Raw, bleeding, foul, noxious things; cured. Sins of omission and commission; mended. Dank hidden deeds; obliterated. Frantic, obscene thoughts – all made well again!

*Toasts* **Tom** *with the tumbler and takes a gulp.*

Christ! No wonder you shouted.

*He quickly sloshes some whisky into the tumbler and swigs it back but the taste is still foul. He gets up and finds* **Tom**'s *feeder cup, unscrews the top, pours whisky into it and takes a drink.*

That's better.

*He places the whisky and the medicine bottles together.*

Quite a nice way to go, don't you think? Pink and amber. Boudoir colours. Oh, God. Regard this, Tom, as a confessional. Will you? Good lad. 'She has been forgiven much, therefore she loves much.' Well, I'm the other side of the coin. I have loved much and therefore I need to be forgiven much. The other side of the coin.

Tails I lose. I did love you, Tom. Christ, how I loved you. That's not right, I do love you. Christ, how I do love you. See?

*He takes a gulp of medicine from the bottle and washes it down with whisky straight from the bottle.*

No. Do it properly. (*Pours the whisky into the cup.*) You are my life and my mind. You are in my waking and in my sleeping. You are in my gut and in my blood and I love you. Love you. (*Another big gulp of whisky. He retches.* **Tom** *is growing more and more agitated.*) It doesn't do you any good if it tastes nice. You're a good lad, Tom, you are. (**Doug** *shivers.*) You cold? You cold, son? You shouldn't be out here in the cold. Here . . . (*Struggles out of the cardigan.*) Have this. (*Drapes it over* **Tom** *clumsily.* **Tom** *is crying now.*) There you are, son. Tell you a secret? Your mother's pills . . . I took them all. One and all. Clever, eh? Not just a pretty face, your old dad. If the booze doesn't get me the happy pills will. Pills will . . . pills will . . . pig's swill. Can't bear them knowing, see. Looking and seeing. All the years come to nothing. All the things they said, over all the years, come to nothing. I wanted to be such a good father, Tom. Such a good . . . Oh, Tom, don't cry. Don't cry. There's a good lad. Nothing to cry for, Tom. Lots and lots of people, Tom. All going to look after you . . . You'll be alright, you'll see. There now, there . . . shhh. Shush. Don't cry, son, don't cry. It's all over, Tom, all over. (**Doug** *appears to fall asleep.* **Tom** *is thrashing wildly now, he cries out.* **Doug** *stirs.*) All the weight and warmth and stink of it . . .

**Doug** *sleeps on to death.* **Tom** *shouts in anguish. He manages to knock* **Doug**'s *knee.* **Doug**'s *head slumps. Gradually* **Tom** *quietens, wide-eyed with grief.*

*Slow fade.*

# The Steward of Christendom
## *by Sebastian Barry*

This is a play about the way history shapes small destinies. It is set in a turbulent period of Irish history between 1922, when the British finally withdrew from Southern Ireland, and 1932, after the murder of nationalist hero Michael Collins.

The play's central character is Thomas Dunne, a solitary latter-day Lear confined to a madhouse by one of his three daughters. Thomas is in his seventies, once a large man now whittled by age. His accent tells us he is from County Wicklow. At the height of his powers he was chief superintendent of the Dublin Metropolitan Police responsible for Dublin Castle itself, his heart and blood pledged to the British cause. He had three hundred men under him to keep the streets of Dublin orderly and safe. An outsider. A Catholic in a British uniform. Stripped of uniform and status after British surrender, life has lost its meaning and his disordered mind is tormented by memories and ghosts from the past.

After a violent outburst in his cell, Thomas is restrained in a straitjacket (although you could probably abandon this for your audition). From the bed he describes a meeting with the charismatic Michael Collins. It is the moment when everything changed for Thomas. The British had been routed. Collins is presented as an elemental force sweeping away the old order, Thomas with it, and plunging Ireland into ruin and chaos. His evocation is so powerful that Collins almost walks from the pages. But the tension between Thomas's Irishness and loyalty to the British Crown is the theme on which the speech hinges and the anomaly at the core of Thomas's character that he tries to make sense of here.

———————

**Thomas** (*from the bed*) I could scarce get over the sight of him. He was a black-haired handsome man, but with the big face and body of a boxer. He would have made a tremendous policeman in other days. He looked to me like Jack Dempsey, one of those prize-fighting men we admired. I would have been proud to have him as my son. When he walked he was sort of dancing, light on his pins, like a good bulleter. Like Patrick O'Brien himself. He looked like he might have given Patrick O'Brien a good challenge for his money on some evening road somewhere, hoisting that ball of granite. He had glamour about him, like a man that goes about with the fit-ups, or one of those picture stars that came on the big ship from New York, to visit us, and there'd be crowds in the streets like for royalty, and it would be a fierce job to keep them held back. Big American men and women, twice the size of any Irish person. And some of them Irish too, but fed those many years on beef and wild turkeys. He was like that, Mr Collins. I felt rough near him, that cold morning, rough, secretly. There never was enough gold in that uniform, never. I thought too, as I looked at him, of my father, as if Collins could have been my son and could have been my father. I had risen as high as a Catholic could go, and there wasn't enough braid, in the upshot. I remembered my father's anger when I failed at my schooling, and how he said he'd put me into the police, with the other fools of Ireland. I knew that by then most of the men in my division were for Collins, that they would have followed him wherever he wished, if he had called them. And for an instant, as the Castle was signed over to him, I felt a shadow of that loyalty pass across my heart. But I closed my heart instantly against it. We were to have peace. On behalf of the Crown the chief secretary wished him well. And indeed it was peaceful, that moment. The savagery and ruin that soon followed broke my heart again and again and again. My streets and squares became places for murder and fire. All that spring and summer, as now and then some brave boy spat at me in the streets, I could not hold back the tide of ruin. It was a personal matter. We had restored order in the days of Larkin. One morning I met a man in St Stephen's Green. He was looking at a youngster thrown half in under a bush. No more than eighteen. The man himself was one of that army of ordinary, middle-class Irishmen with firm views and moustaches. He was apoplectic. We looked at each other. The birds were singing pleasantly, the early sun was up. 'My grandsons,' he said, 'will be feral in this garden – mark my words.'

# The Overgrown Path *by Robert Holman*

**The Overgrown Path** is set on a Greek Island in 1984. Dr Daniel Howarth is a big, broad-shouldered man in his early seventies who lives on the island with his much-loved wife, Beth. Daniel is the son of a self-educated labour activist from Manchester. A brilliant mind took him to Cambridge where he led the research into the development of the hydrogen bomb. Think how his education might impact on his northern vowels. Only after the bombing of Nagasaki did he realise the appalling implications of his research.

In this scene he and Beth have returned to the island from Japan after meeting Etsuko, a Japanese woman whom Beth befriended while working with the American Red Cross relief team in Nagasaki during the war. Etsuko only escaped harm because she was swimming under water when the bomb fell. This meeting has enabled Daniel to apologise for his role in these events and find a degree of resolution.

In this scene Daniel is talking to Nicholas on the beach. Nicholas has come from England to interview him for his Ph.D. thesis on 'How chance has changed history'. He has discovered Daniel is his father and is asking some penetrating questions.

This is a terrible time for Daniel. Beth is dying of leukaemia and their daughter, Sarah, has been killed by a random flash of lightning and is soon to be buried on the island.

In this speech Daniel tells Nicholas about his path from the first clear-eyed days of scientific discovery to the more tangled rationale for continuing his work during the war and afterwards (the overgrown path of the title). It is an explanation rather than a justification but Daniel's shaking hand and frequent pauses as he puffs on his cigarette, gathering and weighing his thoughts, betray the huge pressure he is under. Daniel is a deeply moral man. He has taken full responsibility for his actions and has been coping with the guilt ever since. He has come to understand that his quest for knowledge has led him to tamper with things at the very root of existence, and betray the legacy of his father's ideal. Nicholas's questions elicit much more than he expects.

---

**Daniel** (*picking up his jacket*) My father was a docker. A unionist, an agitator.

*He takes a packet of cigarettes and a box of matches from the pocket. He puts the jacket down.*

When they sacked him I must have been in my early teens. You were right, we did go without shoes for a while.

*He lights a cigarette.*

My father was a stoic. A great educationalist. He read the Co-op library from cover to cover. When he died there were over a thousand people at his funeral. There's a school named after him in Manchester. The William Howarth School.

*He throws the cigarette packet and the box of matches on to his jacket.*

He taught us that learning meant dignity. He was wrong, of course. How I wish I'd been a plumber, or an electrician.

*He puffs on his cigarette.*

When I left Manchester Grammar School I worked for a company which specialised in making laboratory equipment. I was nineteen, twenty, twenty-two. Eventually, kindly, they saw me through Cambridge. Can you imagine how exciting those years were? Mingling with the best, beating them.

*He puffs on his cigarette.*

To use your analogy, the path of atomic physics seemed clear. I just walked along it. No, strode arrogantly. I envy you your intelligence. We knew it was important. Obviously, we did. How much d'you ever know the consequences of something which isn't yet finished? The pattern comes later. We were aware it had implications, yes we were. And we knew research of a very similar kind was going on all over Europe. And America.

*His hand is shaking slightly. He puffs on his cigarette.*

I was a junior then, don't forget. It wasn't until the war – the war escalated the whole bloody damn thing. When the government finally realised what had been going on – well, that was it, it was out of our hands. Correspondence with Europe stopped. The Americans moved into Los Alamos.

*His hand is shaking.*

In nineteen forty-five we were frightened that Hitler would get there first.

*He puffs on his cigarette. He is speaking more quietly.*

And after the war, well – for the same reasons we'd been frightened of Germany, we were now scared stiff of the Russians. For all we knew, Russia already had an atom bomb.

*A slight pause.*

So I went on working, Nicholas.

*A slight pause.*

Most of my real work was done on the hydrogen bomb in the fifties. Though that's not important. It was too late by then. As you should know, knowledge has its own momentum. It's unstoppable. That's what my father didn't understand.

# Dead White Males *by David Williamson*

This is a satire on political correctness and academic pseudary. It is set on the campus of New West University in Western Australia and in the home of the Judd family.

Col Judd has just passed his seventy-seventh birthday. He is dying of cancer. All his life he has worked hard running a roofing company to support his family, for which they have shown little thanks. It was punishing work that has left him with constant back pain. There is no love lost between Col and his family who perceive him as a mean authoritarian bully and variously lay the blame for their unhappy lives at his feet.

In this scene his feminist granddaughter Angela, a student of 'literary theory' at New West, has been dispatched to investigate the dominant patriarchal influences and controlling ideologies in her family. She has come to interview Col for her university dissertation. From her perspective Col is an old dinosaur – 'unreconstructed', chauvinistic, sexist and conservative. She arrives full of preconceptions, feminist dogma and family prejudice but as she learns more about family history from Col's point of view, her rigid notions begin to crumble.

Here Col tells Angela how he views his life in retrospect. He doesn't pull his punches. After all he has nothing left to lose. His response to Angela's questioning is bluff and uncompromising. He talks from the hip. No frills. No obfuscation. He has no time for Angela's feminist theories. This is the real world. He did what he had to do. Far from being the monster of family mythology, he emerges as a man of principle, committed to doing the right thing in spite of the sacrifices involved, a child of his generation driven by the practical realities of supporting wife and child in the face of hardship and injury.

The speech leads to the revelation that for the last fifteen years Col has secretly been giving financial support to the family of his partner who was more seriously disabled at work. It's a gesture of generosity and quiet heroism that completely deconstructs Angela's preconceptions and the rigid theories she had sought to apply.

**Col** You said you wanted to know how I view my life in retrospect? You really want to know? OK. My life was tremendous, right up to the time I married your grandmother. Cricket, football, billiards, dances, mates, motorbikes, the odd beer and a dead easy job – working for the council. Paradise. Then along comes this pretty little bit of fluff, butter wouldn't melt in her mouth, just wanted to please my every whim – hah, what a sucker I was. Suddenly – I'm married, but before I even get to find out what a tough little nut your grandma really is, along comes the Second World War. So of course a bloke does the right thing and finds himself facing the invincible Imperial Japanese Army on the Kokoda trail. Now I'm not going to tell you what I went through up there, because I can hardly bear thinking about it even now. Most of my mates died, but I survived. Point one for your bloody feminist theories – when there's a war on and some poor fools have got to go it's blokes who get sent. And don't tell me it's the women who get raped because there wasn't any raping going on up there on the trail. All that was happening was that I was either delirious with malaria or getting shot at. OK, I get home from the war and the minute I climb into bed your grandma is pregnant with your father. No pill in those days. She stops working and my council job is paid nowhere near enough for my new responsibilities. The only way to make enough money is to do some job that's so tough that not many others will do it. Like most of your sex you'll end up sitting on your bum somewhere working at a desk, so you'll never get to understand what it's like to lug millions of tiles up on to thousands of roofs, year in year out starting at five every morning. And when you're up there you know that one day, sooner or later, you're going to have your one bad fall. So you always take on a partner so you can help each other out with money when your time comes. I had my big one when I was in my early thirties. In hospital for three weeks but luckily, except for a back that was agony from there on in, I was more or less intact. The doctor said I should never have to go up on roofs again the back was so bad – three fused vertebrae – but by this time I had three kids. Point two for you feminists. If a bloke has kids he's the one who finally has to earn the dough.

# Acknowledgements

All plays published by Methuen except where otherwise stated. Any enquiries regarding performance rights should be made to the authors' agents as listed below.

pp 7–9 extract from *Goliath* copyright © by Bryony Lavery 1997 c/o The Peters, Fraser and Dunlop Group Ltd, Drury House, 34–43 Russell Street, London WC2B 5HA.

With special thanks to Berseford Leroy MSC for writing The Don's rap.

pp 12–13 extract from *The Shadow of a Boy* © by Gary Owen 2002 c/o ICM Ltd, 76 Oxford Street, London W1D 1BS.

pp 14–15 extract from *The Body* © by Nick Darke 1983 c/o ICM Ltd, 76 Oxford Street, London W1D 1BS.

pp 16–17 extract from *Ting Tang Mine* © by Nick Darke 1987, 1999 c/o ICM Ltd, 76 Oxford Street, London W1D 1BS.

pp 20–21 extract from *Eden* © by Eugene O'Brien 2001 c/o Curtis Brown Ltd, Haymarket House, 28–9 Haymarket, London SW1Y 4SP.

p 24 extract from *Roberto Zucco* © Les Éditions Minuit 1990. Translation copyright © 1997 by Martin Crimp c/o Judy Daish Associates Ltd, 2 St Charles Place, London W10 6EG.

p 26 extract from *Bloody Poetry* copyright © 1985, 1988, 1989 by Howard Brenton c/o Casarotto Ramsay & Associates Ltd, National House, 60–66 Wardour Street, London W1V 4ND.

p 28 extract from *Shopping and Fucking* © by Mark Ravenhill 1996, 2001. Translation copyright © 1997 by Martin Crimp, 2001 c/o Casarotto Ramsay & Associates Ltd, National House, 60–66 Wardour Street, London W1V 4ND.

pp 32-3 extract from *A Jamaican Airman Foresees His Death* © by Fred D'Aguiar 1995 c/o Curtis Brown Ltd, Haymarket House, 28–9 Haymarket, London SW1Y 4SP.

pp 36–7 extract from *A Vision of Love Revealed in Sleep* © by Neil Bartlett 1990 c/o Simon Mellor, Lyric Theatre, Hammersmith, King Street, London W6 0QL.

p 39 extract from *Other People* © by Christopher Shinn 2000 c/o The Gersh Agency, 41 Madison Avenue, 33rd Floor, New York, New York, 10010, USA.

p 42–3 extract from *Six Degrees of Separation* © by John Guare 1990, 1992. Used by permission of Vintage Books, a division of Random House, Inc. c/o ICM 40 West 57th Street, New York, NY 10019, USA.

p 45 extract from *A Lie of the Mind* © Sam Shepard 1986 and 1987; for repertory and production rights contact Josef Weinberger Ltd (aka Warner/Chappell Plays Ltd) 12–14 Mortimer Street, London W1T 3JJ.

pp 48–9 extract from *Cigarettes and Chocolate* © by Anthony Minghella 1989 c/o Judy Daish Associates Ltd, 2 St Charles Place, London W10 6EG.

p 51 extract from *Alphabetical Order* © by Michael Frayn 1977, 1985 c/o The Peters, Fraser and Dunlop Group Ltd, Drury House, 34–43 Russell Street, London WC2B 5HA.

p 53 extract from *Closer* © by Patrick Marber 1997, 1999 c/o Judy Daish Associates Ltd, 2 St Charles Place, London W10 6EG.

p 55 extract from *Humble Boy*. First published by Faber and Faber 2001, copyright © by Charlotte Jones c/o Peters Fraser and Dunlop Group Ltd, Drury House, 34–43 Russell Street, London WC2B 5HA.

pp 58–9 extract from *Foley* by Michael West 2001 c/o Judy Daish Associates Ltd, 2 St Charles Place, London W10 6EG.

pp 60–1 extract from *The Censor* © by Anthony Neilson 1997 c/o Julia Tyrrell Management, 55 Fairbridge Road, London N19 3EW.